The LIVING WORD

Also by Harold Klemp

MAHANTA

This book has been authored by and published under the supervision of the Mahanta, the Living ECK Master, Sri Harold Klemp. It is the Word of ECK.

The LIVING WORD

BOOK 4

HAROLD KLEMP

ECKANKAR
Minneapolis
www.Eckankar.org

The Living Word, Book 4

Copyright © 2019 ECKANKAR

Printed in USA

Library of Congress Control Number: 89-086022
ISBN: 978-1-57043-469-3

Compiled by Jane Burgess
Edited by Patrick Carroll, Joan Klemp, and Eric Wollan
Author photo by Art Galbraith
Text illustrations by Cynthia Samul

∞ This paper meets the requirements of ANSI/NISO Z39.48-1992 (Permanence of Paper).

CONTENTS

See also Story Index on page 287

FOREWORD

The teachings of ECK define the nature of Soul. You are Soul, a particle of God sent into the worlds (including earth) to gain spiritual experience.

The goal in ECK is spiritual freedom in this lifetime, after which you become a Co-worker with God, both here and in the next world. Karma and reincarnation are primary beliefs.

Key to the ECK teachings is the Mahanta, the Living ECK Master. He has the special ability to act as both the Inner and Outer Master for ECK students. The prophet of Eckankar, he is given respect but is not worshipped. He teaches the sacred name of God, HU. When sung just a few minutes each day, HU will lift you spiritually into the Light and Sound of God—the ECK (Holy Spirit). This easy spiritual exercise and others will purify you. You are then able to accept the full love of God in this lifetime.

Sri Harold Klemp is the Mahanta, the Living ECK Master today. Author of many books, discourses, and articles, he teaches the ins and outs of the spiritual life. Many of his talks are available to you on audio and video recordings. His teachings lift people and help them recognize and understand their own experiences in the Light and Sound of God.

The Living Word, Book 4, is a collection of articles he wrote from 2006 to 2018. Ranging from basic to more esoteric ECK teachings, they show how to find spiritual freedom by bringing experiences with the Light and Sound of God into your everyday life.

To find out more about Harold Klemp and Eckankar, please turn to page 275 in the back of this book.

Divine love and intelligence—the ECK—is always at work among us. Look for Its dealings.

CHAPTER ONE

Love's Golden Thread

1
Love Is a Many-Splendored Thing

"*K*eep away from people who try to belittle your ambitions," said Mark Twain, humorist and writer. "Small people always do that, but the really great make you feel that you, too, can become great."

Magnanimity on that order is a demonstration of love. Good friends will do that. It is as natural to them as breathing, because they want to help you realize your dreams and, in doing so, let you discover a measure of your godlike qualities and turn up your lamp to let a little more light brighten this world.

Love, truly, makes the world go around.

In fact, a capacity to love is the very quality that attracts a seeker to the Mahanta, the Living ECK Master. One who finds him is often poor and humble, not in good health. Of note is that the Master loves the seeker more than the seeker loves his own impurities.

Love is a many-splendored thing. It is reflected in every part of life, from the Maker's creation of the universes to the affinity that exists even

A capacity to love is the very quality that attracts a seeker to the Mahanta, the Living ECK Master.

among the smallest creatures that abide there.

Love is a golden thread.

Love is generally thought of as being of two kinds: detached love and warm love. The first is goodwill or charity. This is what we give to all people outside our immediate circle of family and friends.

Second is warm love. People are capable of giving only a limited amount of it, no matter what they believe. The reason is that it also involves the giving of small considerations to those within their close circle, like a tender hug or kiss, giving help and encouragement, sharing duties at home, sympathizing at some setback, and being kind and considerate.

It further means holding our tongue when there is a misunderstanding or a difference of opinion between us and our loved ones.

Yet there is a third kind of love, spiritual love.

Another name for divine love is the ECK, the Music of God.

Spiritual love is of the highest nature, the love of an individual for the Mahanta, the Living ECK Master. He is the manifestation of God's love. Another name for divine love is the ECK, Holy Spirit. It is rightfully called the Voice of God, too, for It speaks to our spiritual Self.

Still another name for the ECK is the Music of God. It, along with the Divine Light, is central to one's spiritual life.

The holy book of Eckankar, *The Shariyat-Ki-Sugmad*, Book One, tells how the ECK Sound Current is often weak at first. However, the Master gives a student unique methods to begin opening the Spiritual Eye. As it opens, the Sound becomes ever clearer, more distinct, more compelling, a magnet of love.

This divine music then begins to draw Soul higher. The journey home to God may now proceed in earnest.

The special methods the Master gives to a lover of God are the Spiritual Exercises of ECK. Many, many are available in the outer works of Eckankar. Moreover, the Master will also pass along others in the dream state or contemplation. The latter match one's state of consciousness. The experiences that accrue from them are, like the outer exercises, designed to refine one spiritually.

Giving love must necessarily begin at home. If you can love those near and dear to you, then you are well on your way to loving God.

In sum, *The Shariyat*, in Book Two, says that "love, faith, and humility are the virtues which must first be established in the seeker before he can come unto the Mahanta, the Living ECK Master."

God's love, you come to find, is surely a many-splendored thing.

This divine music begins to draw Soul higher.

2
Life Deals Our
Cards Facedown

*T*his title, for ECK chelas in a culture where card playing is not done, means that usually people don't know what is on today's spiritual menu.

"Card playing" and "spiritual menu" is a mixed metaphor, but it's a way to pose two provocative issues: Who knows the future, short of the present succumbing to it in time? And why does a given event occur now, of all times?

Why does a given event occur now, of all times?

Remember, life's lessons are to teach, not to punish one. That is a spiritual view of good and bad karma.

"John" is from Africa. At the time, he was living in a rented apartment. The people next door practiced poor hygiene, so soldier ants were common pests there. However, they never bothered John.

That changed one day. He unwittingly asked the divine dealer (the ECK) for another card (lesson). Then the fun began.

One morning, he went outside to the building's refuse container and saw heaps of soldier ants there. He decided to do everyone a favor and burn them. It was a job well done.

But at five o'clock the next morning, he awoke to ants on his bed. Ants were everywhere. Outside his door it was even worse. He fought them for two hours, using over ten liters (two and a half gallons) of kerosene and rags and newspapers.

All to no avail.

Ants were trooping into his apartment by the thousands or millions. He'd never seen such numbers.

John understood then that this invasion was retribution for yesterday. They'd come to teach him a lesson, and he was learning fast.

Soldier ants had come to teach John a lesson, and he was learning fast.

He immediately began to sing *HU*. At the same time, he apologized to the ants, aloud. He pleaded in human language. Passersby thought his behavior odd. He said he was sorry for what he'd done the previous day, not recognizing that they, too, needed the freedom to live and do as they pleased.

"Please forgive me!"

As he continued begging, a wonderful thing happened. The ants turned around. They retraced their journey back to where they'd come from, the bush.

In less than twenty minutes, the entire army had disappeared.

So when the divine dealer turned up the card relating to this experience, John received a reminder that animals are Soul too.

"Lissa" is a psychologist who took a job working with autistic children. The job was a card dealt facedown. But life, the divine dealer, had hidden an unexpected twist to her story, which she would discover later.

Her job entails a lot of lifting. One day, she suffered a painful back injury that kept her from work. So she was unable to be with the children, which greatly distressed her.

Could she do a job like this, with all the lifting and pulling?

Finally, she was back at work, among the kids again. But all their screaming and crying began to get on her nerves. She confided in her mom.

"Remember," her mom said, "crying is the HU."

Lissa now also remembered how children are often so close to God.

The next day, she got to work with a boy she had liked from the start. But her accident had kept her from spending much time with him. He had many problems at home, and she wanted to comfort him.

Autistic children need help going to the bathroom, and other things. After they finished cleaning up, she heard him babbling, so she imitated him, trying to communicate.

Many of her children cannot talk or say real words.

Hearing her babble like him, he walked over. Then he wrapped his arms around her neck.

At that moment, clear as a bell, he said, "I like that."

Awestruck, Lissa repeated his words back to him. They had actually communicated! This marked a major breakthrough, even though the boy immediately relapsed into babbling. At this moment, she realized, they had recognized one another as Soul. He had addressed her concerns about whether to continue in this line of work. Yes, she did need to continue; she was helping him.

Awestruck, Lissa repeated the autistic boy's words back to him. They had actually communicated!

Love helps us through our dark nights of Soul.

His unexpected few words were Lissa's card turned faceup. An unexpected future had revealed itself. A card turned over.

So, we may be shown the future. And a given incident occurs when we are ready to move into an expanded state of consciousness.

Love helps us through our dark nights of Soul.

3
A Shake-Up, Caffeine, and Some Birds

*S*tories about these three subjects are related in neither time nor space. One is from a Nigerian; the second, a Canadian; the third, a US woman from the Midwest. Their stories also drew from events months apart.

Yet they illustrate a common bond.

All show the workings of the Holy Spirit in one's everyday life. But they often go unnoticed. Each of these workings does carry with it a lesson, if we have the awareness and humility to receive it.

"Jacob" is a Nigerian. He had done business with a government agency months earlier, but pay for his work was slow in coming. It came to him then to try a creative exercise of ECK. He imagined Wah Z and other ECK Masters wielding brooms, sweeping the cobwebs in the building, office by office. This exercise took some time.

Then he put it completely out of his mind. The ECK would do what the ECK would do. It was that simple.

The unimaginable happened a few days later. There was massive shake-up at the agency, as the

It came to Jacob to try a creative exercise of ECK. He imagined ECK Masters sweeping the cobwebs, office by office.

government acted to remove all the corrupt heads. Top management staff were let go; new managers were appointed. The latter set about a reorganization. Senior staff under them were redeployed.

Time has passed, but still Jacob awaits payment. Why? What was his lesson in this?

He admits to smugness in being a channel for the changes that took place at the agency. He relished his role. Where was the humility? Yet Jacob will be made right when that lesson sinks in.

Our second story sees a Canadian on vacation. "Mary's" story had begun three years earlier, when she asked the Mahanta for help to stop drinking coffee. She sensed it was harmful to her health.

So at a store while on vacation, she saw an energy drink for sale. She got a nudge to buy one. The label stated that the contents were full of vitamins.

A few days later, she drank it.

Poor timing, she later decided, because that very morning she had downed three cups of strong coffee.

She went to the pool. There, she began to feel queasy, but the feeling would surely pass. Instead, after an hour or so, she felt worse, much worse. Should she return to her apartment or seek medical help? She said to a desk clerk, "I am sick. Can you find someone to help me?" Mary was frightened.

The clerk spoke no English. He hurried away to locate someone who did. A man nearby had overheard her plea.

"I am a doctor," he said. "Can I help you?" He felt her pulse; it was fast. "Did you have an energy drink today?" Mary said yes.

Mary was frightened. A man nearby overheard. "I am a doctor," he said. "Can I help you?"

The doctor mused, "A fast diagnosis I made." He seemed surprised and happy it had so easily come to mind. He said the drink was high in caffeine, and that Mary was suffering from palpitations.

The doctor understood her anxiety.

"It is very important to drink a lot of water and lie down," he instructed. "Your palpitations will pass." Mary thanked him, and the doctor left.

After a while, she threw up. And shortly, she felt her old self again.

It struck her that this was the first time in her life that she had ever had this kind of drink, yet the doctor immediately knew the problem. The hand of the Master was apparent here, even three years after her request for help in overcoming this dependency on caffeine.

Story three is about three baby birds and their mother.

"Carol" says they apparently had a nest nearby. The mother had led them to Carol's balcony, where her son had placed a bird feeder on a nearby wall.

The mother flew up to the feeder, but its feeding tray was empty. Evidently, she had hoped to scratch seeds from the feeder to her chicks below. Unfazed, she studied the problem. There must be a way to dislodge the jammed seeds and refill the tray. It meant prying up the lid.

Her plan was pretty good. She wedged her beak under the lid, opened the lid, and hopped into the feeder. Unfortunately, the lid dropped down again, trapping her inside.

This remarkable mother had a plan for escape, however.

The hand of the Master was apparent here, even three years after her request for help overcoming dependency on caffeine.

She chattered to her chicks with firm orders. They understood.

Meanwhile, inside, Carol was absorbed in reading. The solitude of her home was abruptly broken by loud cries of cheep, cheep, cheep. The chicks had come to the balcony door and were looking up at her in the living room, wanting her to follow them.

Outside, she spotted their trapped mother and immediately freed her. The obedient children were thus instrumental in rescuing their mom.

The lesson borne by all three stories is that divine love and intelligence—the ECK—is always at work among us.

Look for Its dealings.

Divine love and intelligence—the ECK—is always at work among us. Look for Its dealings.

4
Explorations in a Rocking Chair

*T*he most useful, but unrecognized, gift to mankind is the Spiritual Exercises of ECK. They are the highest form of exploration there is.

Explorations are of three kinds: geographical, mental, and spiritual. In a real sense, a common thread runs through all of them, for behind each is a driving force that urges an explorer to satisfy his curiosity about some new region. So the difference that separates the three kinds of exploration is simply a matter of degree.

In truth, what are they but different states of consciousness?

J. Allen Boone, the author of *Kinship with All Life*, wrote another book, *Letters to Strongheart*. The first book details the life of a wonder dog, Strongheart. This dog was once an actor in the movies. He left audiences in awe, because he performed feats that led people to wonder seriously if some animals were smarter than humans.

Boone had the good fortune to work closely with Strongheart. The two, after a rocky time of getting to know one another, soon became fast friends.

The Spiritual Exercises of ECK are the highest form of exploration there is.

15

Then Strongheart translated.

Even so, Boone knew there is no death as people normally think of it. There was no question in his mind that Strongheart was alive and well, yet now in a new world of being.

So Boone wrote him a series of letters that served as a means for Boone to continue his heart-to-heart discussions with Strongheart. Each letter had a theme. In it, Boone would tell of his observations about people and things he encountered in his travels. These were then published as *Letters to Strongheart*.

One of his letters tells of an unusual man he once had the good fortune to meet in Shanghai, China.

Boone attended a reception for a distinguished traveler who was soon to leave for the Gobi Desert. In attendance were other explorers, all of whom were ready to join any venture that turned up, and Boone moved from room to room to listen in on their tales of daring adventures.

In one of the corners of the main room, he spotted an interesting-looking man seated alone. Boone introduced himself. After some small talk, he asked the man where the most interesting adventures could be found at the present time.

This man came to realize that the real unexplored oceans and lands were all inside him.

The other studied him, then said, "My personal preference is for sitting in an old-fashioned rocking chair."

It turned out that this man was himself an explorer. He had been to all the out-of-the-way places, but he came to realize that the real unexplored oceans and lands were all inside him.

So he meditated. More properly, he preferred to call it mental exploring.

But why the rocking chair?

Everything, he explained, is in a continuous state of motion, or vibration. Most people try to ignore this fact and attempt to disregard it, thinking that, as individuals, they can move about the universes doing as they please. However, this is a misguided notion of what it means to be a law unto oneself.

The rocker helped him overcome that tendency. Whenever he planned to explore his inner worlds, he began to rock gently, bringing himself into harmony with the cosmic rhythm. And he also slowed his breathing.

All the while, he pictured his thoughts moving ever outward. He soon lost the sense of being tied to his human body and was thus able to soar free in spirit, at liberty to explore the wonders of his very own magnificent worlds.

That is what the rocking chair helped him to achieve.

He was thus able to soar free in spirit, at liberty to explore the wonders of his very own magnificent worlds.

*   *   *

This book of Boone's, like his other, is far in advance of today's general state of consciousness. It was republished in 1977, a fitting complement to *Kinship with All Life*, copyrighted in 1954, which heralded a new level of thinking about the wide possibilities of consciousness. The new edition of *Letters to Strongheart* then came along like a footnote. It enriches a reader's understanding of the workings of consciousness as shown in the observations of a special man, J. Allen Boone.

His explorations, like those of the man with the rocking chair, can only range up to and through the mental planes. Both of these individuals will,

When a certain method seems no longer to work, go and explore. Look for a new one. Another will show up.

sooner than later, come upon a whole new creation of worlds. These are the true spiritual worlds.

The rocking chair as an aid to contemplation is another of many ways to approach the doing of your spiritual exercises.

The Mahanta, the Living ECK Master offers all kinds of ways to approach the Spiritual Exercises of ECK. When a certain method shows results, repeat it. When that way seems no longer to work, go and explore. Look for a new one.

Another will show up.

5
Is There a Fresh Way to Say . . . ?

*I*s there a fresh way to say the Spiritual Exercises of ECK are your lifeline to the divine power? Undoubtedly. But the key is always in the actual doing, not just the saying.

"Bill" had a sudden run of bad luck at home while he was away on a trip. When he returned, he found someone had flattened his mailbox. The courier had no way to deliver the mail. Also, no internet access. So his email was also in limbo. To get it, he carted his laptop to his workplace, but for some unknown reason, the power company had cut off service, so the router didn't work.

No internet connection there either.

What on earth?

The years had impressed upon him that nothing ever happened without a reason. No mail at home. No email at home or the office. At bottom, no communication.

Finally, he saw the connection.

Work, family, home, and even his ECK duties had led to a neglect of his spiritual exercises. He

What on earth? No mail at home. No email at home or the office. Finally, Bill saw the connection.

immediately resumed them, at the same time every day.

Shoring up his spiritual life still more, he began to listen to ECK audiobooks in his vehicle while driving for his job. He further reminded himself to place full attention on Divine Spirit during the day, with love and much devotion.

The greatest result of this lesson, Bill says, is learning the importance of his communication with the Holy Spirit.

It is a reciprocal relationship. Trust the ECK and communicate with It, for that leads to being a better ECK channel.

Is there a fresh way to say the Spiritual Exercises of ECK are vital, even life-preserving?

So, is there a fresh way to say the Spiritual Exercises of ECK are vital, even life-preserving? Let's ask "John" and his wife, "Sara," from Nigeria, who have four children. Sara was not yet an ECK-ist. Nevertheless, John started a family HU song with their children.

Sara runs a clothes-making shop only a short walk from home. As you'll see, this point is important. In any case, a customer was expecting an article of clothing as soon as possible. But a girl who usually works there failed to show up.

So Sara found herself alone in the shop.

She tried one sewing machine, then another, a third, and a fourth, but all proved inoperable. Nor was either of the two repairmen she called on available that day. She was hemmed in, so to speak. "God," she cried, "if you don't want me to work today, I'm going home to rest."

A crucial decision, it turned out.

Long story short, at home she rested in the living room with children home that day. A daughter, wanting to use the gas cooker, came to complain the fuel was gone. Sara gave her money for kerosene. But when the girl returned, Sara noticed the dealer had mistakenly supplied the wrong fuel, the highly volatile petrol instead of kerosene.

Lighting petrol would have ended in serious injury or even death.

The family enjoys the Mahanta's protection. On this occasion, he stayed the karma that otherwise would have come due.

Is there a fresh way to say . . . ?

The Mahanta stayed the karma that otherwise would have come due.

These people we have come to call Lemurians were good people in the finest sense, without the ambition to want or take that which was another's.

CHAPTER TWO

Spiritual History Lessons

6
Peace in Our Time— or Ever?

*R*evised history has it that the American Indian tribes of olden times were a nice bunch of fellows, at peace with one another and with themselves.

Yet the truth is a far different matter.

In the early seventeenth century, the Five Nations of Indians dominated other tribes in Canada and the American Northeast. The Five Nations was a confederacy of some, though not all, Iroquoian tribes. Their enemies counted among their number other Iroquoian tribes like the Huron and Tobacco tribes. These latter scorned the tribes of the Five Nations. They loved to do battle with them.

The Indians of the Old West were of the same stripe. Combat with an enemy gave the young men of both tribes a chance to demonstrate their valor and thus become braves.

The ferocious Comanches of the Southwest fought other tribes and whites alike. Yet they, too, had a fearsome, though despised, adversary in the Tonkawa Indians, who allied with the Texans. They served as scouts for the Texas Rangers and the

Combat with an enemy gave young men of both tribes a chance to demonstrate their valor and thus become braves.

army. A small tribe, the Tonkawas had joined up with the whites and let them hammer the Comanches. If some of the enemy warriors were killed, the Tonkawas would celebrate the occasion and hold a feast. They cooked and ate the choicest of the dead.

So much for the "gentle souls" of the American Indians.

Speaking of Souls, why is it that men fight each other? Why do ants? And what about two tomcats?

Speaking of Souls, why is it that men fight each other? Why do ants? And what about two tomcats? Two bulls, two roosters, two boars, or two stallions?

The ECK Master Rebazar Tarzs sized it up like this: it is a warring universe.

So what kind of place is this thing called earth?

White tribes in the long-ago times of the United States's North and South once engaged in the awful Civil War. First of all, no "civil" war is ever civil. This war fielded some of the largest and bloodiest engagements the world had ever seen.

Why did they fight? What difference of opinion divided the two sides?

Abraham Lincoln, the US president then, noised it abroad that the Civil War was about the preservation of the Union. The South said it was about its civil rights. But the people of both the North and the South know the real issue: slavery. Should the southern states be allowed to hold slaves? The resulting difference of opinion cost many lives.

What reality lay behind the theater of truth's curtains? It's so simple that many overlook it. No two people share exactly the same state of consciousness.

Not even within groups where one might expect to see "like-minded" people. Members of churches, for example; and families, labor unions, political parties, sports teams, and the list goes on. Conflict destroys peace.

No great civilization in the pages of history was ever successful in developing into maturity without the tempering of some conflict.

The ancient Egyptians were mostly stay-at-home types. They were content to expend their energies in Egypt, so they rarely sent armies on the road to conquer the world, as Alexander the Great later set out to do. There was an exception to the Egyptians' general stay-at-home policy. Periodically, their armies went north to beat up on neighbors like the Edomites and the Moabites. It was to show who was the big rooster in the yard.

The ancient Egyptians periodically went north to beat up on neighbors. It was to show who was the big rooster in the yard.

There was no peace inside nor outside the Egyptian borders.

The ancient Chinese were more aggressive than the Egyptians. Early in China's history, a variety of local lords ran minor kingdoms in the northern and plains areas, as well as farther south. Eventually, the stronger rulers took over their weaker neighbors. The outcome of centuries of intermittent warfare is the China of today.

So, no peace in the world's oldest civilization either.

Europe, too, is no stranger to warfare. Just its wars of religion caused enough mayhem to satisfy even the most bloodthirsty Souls. These conflicts included the French Wars of Religion (1562–98), the Thirty Years' War (1618–48), and the English Civil Wars (1642–51), which pitted Protestants against the Catholics.

And northern Asia, under the Russian czars and the Soviet Union, could only dream of peace.

There was little of it.

Many, it seems, take pleasure in telling their fellows what to do and how to do it. The solution, if one is even possible considering this world of imperfect beings, would be for everyone who wants things to change, to first change himself for the better.

Until that happens, there won't be peace in our time, or ever. Peace begins in the heart.

With that said, however, there is a bright side to what would otherwise be a rather gloomy picture. We certainly are in this world, but it is possible to rise above it via the Spiritual Exercises of ECK.

Put your attention on the face of the Mahanta, the Living ECK Master and do a short contemplation. Seat yourself comfortably or lie down on your back. Then sing the word *HU*, an ancient name for God. Sing this name for ten or fifteen minutes, either silently or aloud.

This spiritual exercise is a way to enter a higher consciousness and find peace in your heart.

Do this exercise anytime you feel the need for spiritual upliftment. And pay attention to any images or thoughts that may present themselves.

This world can be anything but peaceful, but the spiritual exercise above is a way to enter into a higher state of consciousness and find peace in your heart.

7
Lemuria, Atlantis, and Today

Ages ago, two great civilizations existed on Earth: Lemuria and Atlantis. Their thoughts, beliefs, and actions cast long shadows that reach even to the present day.

Lemuria was the elder of the two civilizations. It was a remarkable land that may be said to belong to the golden age of mankind's history. Its people had come to Earth in obedience to the Maker's dictum for these spirit forms to leave the comforts of the heavens and descend into this world. This place had a much coarser vibration than they had ever known. Nevertheless, these spirits came gladly, obedient to the Sugmad's command.

And so they tumbled downward, ever downward.

When their falling finally ceased, these spirits found themselves cloaked in heavy, clumsy human forms. Soon, too, they discovered the new sensations of a hungry stomach, the pain of thorns, and the uncomfortable effects of heat and cold.

Moreover, they were bewildered or terrified by the strange beasts and fowl with whom they shared their new home.

Lemuria was a remarkable land that may be said to belong to the golden age of mankind's history.

Primitive man had everything to learn.

Again, ages passed. These immigrants from the spirit realms had long since learned ways to express and so develop means to practice the Law of the One. This law simply said to help one's neighbor help himself, for he was of the same essence as you.

These immigrants from the spirit realms learned to practice the Law of the One—to help one's neighbor help himself, for he was of the same essence as you.

These people were what we have come to call Lemurians. They were good people in the finest sense, without the ambition to want or take that which was another's. Further, in addition to being exemplars of moral behavior, they were a technologically advanced people. In the Philippines, remnants of rice terraces speak of a time when this single, massive system of terraces was the breadbasket that fed thousands upon thousands of Lemurians.

But how did they protect the rice from the cyclones that periodically bring devastation to the Philippines, an outpost of Lemuria?

These ingenious people, guided by an understanding of divine law, set up two stations with many large crystals on each. The stations were put on two islands some three hundred miles apart. Not by chance were these two places chosen, for they were located in the exact spot where cyclones that could devastate the Philippines saw their origin.

One station acted as the positive pole of a battery, while the other station was the negative pole. These two poles together bled off the energy of a potential cyclone. Thus, the Philippines' rice terraces were preserved.

There are other examples of their superior knowledge of the physical and spiritual laws. They could also prevent earthquakes. A further ability was to cut, then transport through the air massive blocks of hard stone. These master builders would drop them into place. They were set so closely that a knife blade would not fit between them.

In time, though, seismic upheavals made it apparent that Lemuria's days were numbered. So missionaries went to colonies around the world. There, they hid their writings, to ensure that Lemuria's history would live on in the annals of mankind.

Atlantis, in the Atlantic Ocean, some say, was a Lemurian colony too. Its history was very like that of Lemuria in the Pacific Ocean. Both cultures followed the Law of the One.

However, after a while, a materialistically minded group broke from the original body of righteous Atlanteans. This group turned the spiritual values on their head. They were ambitious. They took others' property by legal means, if possible. Or, they took credit for the hard work and achievements of others.

In short, they believed that having more material goods would bring them happiness.

Atlantis also disappeared under the waves like Lemuria. However, the reasons for their respective demises were different. Lemuria's time had simply come. Like an old person, it had enjoyed a long and fruitful life.

Atlantis, by comparison, was like a robust youth brought to an early end through its misuse of crystals and its practice of black magic.

Both civilizations have left us with a legacy. The peace-loving Lemurians' ideal and practice of serving others is one stream of consciousness. They

Both cultures followed the Law of the One. However, a materialistically minded group of Atlanteans turned the spiritual values on their head.

gave freely, expecting no return. Their ethics, for the most part, were of the highest nature. Not so some of the Atlanteans, who forsook the Law of the One and showed their ambition, malice, and greed.

These two streams of love versus power are in our own society. How can you tell them apart in yourself?

These two streams of love versus power are in our own society. They exist at both the macrocosmic and microcosmic levels, in nations as well as individuals. They are the two poles of positive and negative, of good and evil. They vary in strength from time to time.

How can you tell them apart in yourself?

The higher, positive, spiritual stream is in the forefront when you allow others their spiritual freedom. You let people be. You do not, will not, interfere in their lives. Ever. The lower, negative side will seek to micromanage the affairs of others at every opportunity. The cover will be: "I'm doing it for your own good," or some other artifice of the Kal Niranjan (the negative or evil power).

Both streams are alive in you at all times. Do the Spiritual Exercises of ECK. Keep your spiritual line to the Mahanta open today, tomorrow, and every other day too.

Learn from the ancient Lemurians and Atlanteans. Those lessons will stand you in good stead spiritually.

8
Can Karma Be Managed?

character in a John le Carré novel says, "The cause of death is birth."

What a striking way to illustrate the consequences of that old bugaboo karma and its bedfellow, reincarnation. Yet more to the point, however, is there a way to soften the effects of karma? Certainly. Let's look at a couple of examples of how the Mahanta calmed troubled waters for ECKists.

Let's look at how the Mahanta calmed troubled waters for ECKists.

"John" was truly perplexed. For twenty years and counting, he and "Eric" simply could not get along. No reason seemed to exist for the hostility that kept them apart. Both were ECKists. Somehow, they should have been able to resolve their conflict.

There had to be an answer.

John finally tired of this deep gulf of separation between them. So in contemplation he asked the Mahanta for an insight into the karma behind the other chela's thinly veiled hostility. He was attending an ECK seminar at the time. The following night an inner experience rattled him, because it pointed to him as the culprit responsible for the rift.

In a past life, he and Eric had been the closest of friends. An outcome of this closeness was that Eric's family had come to trust him as if he were a member of the family. So it proved a shock when he impregnated the only daughter, an unpardonable affront in that culture. No surprise was it, then, to learn that Eric had sworn to kill him. Family honor was on the line.

John, however, was the stronger of the two, so when Eric rushed him with a machete, it was as simple as 1, 2, 3 to disarm him. In spite of this, Eric refused to yield so easily. After rushing into a nearby building, he burst from it wielding another machete. But he stopped in his tracks at the sight of John ready to defend himself with the confiscated machete in hand. A standoff.

John, though the stronger, didn't press the issue, because he'd been the offender.

A nudge suggested John could agree to let Eric restore his family's honor in the dream state. John agreed.

Days after this inner experience, John asked the Mahanta for help to resolve the karma. The Master responded. A nudge suggested John could agree to let Eric restore his family's honor in the dream state. John agreed.

Two days later, in an inner experience, somebody shot him in the thigh with an arrow. That satisfied the family honor and Eric's need for revenge, because he was the archer.

The breach could now heal.

Our second story sees the Mahanta using another approach to mend a sticky situation in Nigeria for Robert. More than a decade and a half ago, he'd been employed at a construction site. He was new to the ECK teachings and was only dimly aware of the help available through the Inner Master.

During his noon break, he routinely went off-site to contemplate by the seaside, to listen to the roar of the sea while he chimed in with the HU song. The combination of the two produced a beautiful music that filled him with the love and presence of the Master. An idyllic picture.

But there was one dark cloud in this scene.

The site was surrounded by a fence, and to leave the site meant having to go through a gate manned by a gatekeeper. The man harbored an intense dislike for Robert. But no rule said employees had to remain on the grounds during breaks.

At Robert's approach, the gatekeeper's voice would grow shrill, and a heated argument always followed. The man insisted Robert was not to leave through his gate, while Robert assured him he could. Other security men were obliged to intervene on Robert's behalf.

How Robert disliked this daily hassle. It ruined his mood before his spiritual exercise by the sea.

Then an ECKist mentioned he could call on the Mahanta anytime, in any situation. Robert decided to give it a try. As he walked along the dusty road to the gate, he whispered to the Mahanta, "I'm tired of arguing with this man at the gate. Please help me."

He got a strong nudge to sing *HU*.

Chanting quietly as he neared the gate, he was astonished to see the gatekeeper walk straight toward him, face bright and smiling. He embraced Robert. So much joy flowed between them that their eyes welled with tears. They spoke not a word. But from then on they were friends—without words of explanation.

Robert whispered to the Mahanta, "I'm tired of arguing with this man at the gate. Please help me." He got a strong nudge to sing HU.

Robert recalls, "For the first time I realized how close you (the Master) are to me. Just by requesting, karma collapsed in front of me." This experience is ever on his mind, along with all the blessings the Master has brought to him and his family.

9
Pain and Heartache from Long Ago

Stories of past lives can be ever so painful and messy. They may drive us nearly to tears at their telling. The following story is one such.

I've muted and condensed some of the cyclical repetitions. It's heartbreaking when people run in circles, unable to step aside from the karmic bouts they endure, because they don't understand how they were the first cause of their current perplexity.

We'd like to shout, "Open your eyes, why don't you?"

Of course, they don't. It's not time; they've still more to learn. The Law of Karma insists they trudge through the mud of misery until they've settled the account at issue.

Some of our story's details are altered to protect the identities of the people involved.

Mary's son, Sam, had been trouble nearly from day one. In primary school, he was a terror. How many times did Mary and Frank, his father, hear from teachers about his rowdy behavior? Every little while. Sam's behavior turned even more sour

It's heartbreaking when people run in circles, unable to understand how they were the first cause of their current perplexity.

in middle and high school—suspension upon suspension. In the end, school officials ordered him
to leave. They were fed up fooling with him.

The alternate school that followed his expulsion
from high school lasted three months.

Sometime during those years, Frank, the father,
had left Mary. Sam continued his hurtful ways. In
fact, he ramped up his destructive toll by marrying
a childhood sweetheart. His very worried mother
was relieved to see him finally settling down.
Maybe the responsibilities of marriage would make
him a better person. But then, his drinking flared
up again.

She'd further suspected drug use, which he
stoutly denied. Soon after, however, he spent a
night in jail for drug possession.

Worse lay ahead.

Sam's next twenty years witnessed continued
drug and alcohol abuse, with the addition of wife
and child abuse. His now three divorced wives had
all ignored Mary's pointed advice to leave him, to
curtail more suffering. Ultimately, each, in turn,
dropped him.

What lay behind all this drawn-out trouble? Mary now looked to the Master for an answer.

Along the way, he'd fathered a sprinkling of
kids, causing them untold pain and heartache.

So what lay behind all this drawn-out trouble?
His three wives had given over their lives to serve
him in spite of his ingratitude. They had been in
a tight circle of helping Sam.

Mary now looked to the Master for an answer.

In contemplation, she asked the Mahanta, the
Inner Master, to let her understand this situation.

The answer, when it came, was such a shock
that she realized she'd not been ready for the truth
earlier.

On the inner, the Master guided her to a small rural farmhouse in Norway or Germany, a long time ago. There, she'd married an aloof farmer, but they seldom spoke. They simply did not like each other. Their union had produced four children. The boy was her son, Sam, in the current life, and the three daughters, his wives.

Mary had been extremely cruel to the boy, because he looked too much like his father. Sam got all the dirty chores, and she did not provide him with decent clothing. Often, when she had neglected to feed him, his sisters slipped him food behind her back. This infuriated Mary.

What a tight, karmic band!

The instant she woke from this past life, she cried uncontrollably. How could she ever have been so heartless?

The Mahanta explained, "That's why you've helped him so much in this lifetime, and also the reason the girls have felt so bound to him. Now you can break this karma. He is where he is (facing a prison term) and needs to be. You can no longer help him. He'll be all right. Let the girls be."

There it was, the truth. It will take time to heal her own broken heart, but writing her story to the Outer Master begins her on the road to recovery.

To parrot an old song, "What he has done for others, he'll do for you." The secrets of your yesterdays and todays lie hidden all around, but the Master and the ECK teachings can help you uncover them.

The secrets of your yesterdays and todays lie hidden all around, but the Master and the ECK teachings can help you uncover them.

10

A Structure
to God's Love?

Human love often seems aimless, but, then, so may God's love too. The difference between them is that human love often is aimless, while divine love *always* moves toward some end.

People and events appear to bump into us in haphazard ways. But they are predetermined ways.

If that is the case, however, where is our free will?

Never fear, it is alive and well. Free will operates within a structure, which lets us do what we want to, when we want to, for as long as we want to. But note that even a powerful and important monarch like Louis XIV, of seventeenth- and eighteenth-century France, the "Sun King," could often do as he pleased, but later come to regret it.

He enjoyed a reign of seventy-two years, the longest of any European ruler. Louis was a shrewd man. He built a many-roomed palace at Versailles partly in order to keep a close eye on leading French nobles, whom he "invited" to stay for months at a time.

How could they say no to the king?

Moreover, he was greatly feared by other European monarchs. Louis had a bad habit. He routinely sent his armies into other countries and snatched up some or all of their territory. That did nothing to endear him to his peers.

France had reached the pinnacle of its glory in his day, but already he sensed the seams of his empire begin to unravel.

Late in life, he confided to a friend, "I have loved war too much."

Louis XIV had indeed. Unbridled success it was not, even though his reign saw the expansion of French territory. The gains had come at a great cost. Each time he had ventured out with the intention of a conquest, a coalition of other European powers would align themselves to stop him. He won many battles, but he also lost many others.

All in all, there was a balancing act at play, something far outside Louis XIV's ability to control. You know it as the Law of Karma.

All in all, there was a balancing act at play, something far outside his ability to control. It is called the "balance of power," a political term.

You know it as the Law of Karma.

Napoleon ran into the same iron wall as did Louis, and as have many other rulers over the centuries. Some seem to get away with murder, like Stalin, who enjoyed a natural death. Nonetheless, his time will come. The Lords of Karma will give him other chances in future lives to mend his ways, and, perhaps, even lend him such great power again.

Yet should Stalin choose to rule with brutality, they may still allow it. He is, after all, for all his evil ways, setting into motion currents of energy that speed up the karma of countless people.

But eventually his star will crest and fall from

the heavens too. The power and position will go to another. Neither Stalin nor any other monster can forever escape the Law of Karma and his responsibility to life. For you see, this law is merely a single facet of God's all-embracing love. God's higher law, the Law of Love, operates with a goal of letting us experience ourselves into ever higher states of consciousness.

In the end, the personalities of people like the fearmongers named above will drop away. Those Souls, too, will see purification. And also enlightenment.

The love of God has an underlying structure, indeed.

So much talk about people like the ones above leaves a dirty taste in the mouth. The temptation to say "There but for the grace of God go I" is certainly a strong one. Let me hasten to point out, however, that you, like most chelas, have once also played the role of demon in some long-ago incarnation. There is no reason to take pride in one's humanity. Too many dirt spots soil the cloth of all people.

Still, there is cause for celebration! You are on the path of ECK. So you know what your life is about.

Still, there is cause for celebration!

You are on the path of ECK. You know of the SUGMAD, the ECK, and the Mahanta, the Living ECK Master. So you know what your life is about.

Think back to your days before ECK. Often there was a feeling of loneliness, emptiness, or sadness.

Remember?

Yes, there is an end, a goal, a resting place. You are headed there. Stay the course. Share the good news of ECK with others, for there are many more waiting and searching as you once did.

Be an instrument for God's love. Help others find ECK!

As you have now seen, there *is* a structure to God's love. It embraces you and every other being in existence. Do all you can to live a life of thanks.

Read ECK stories with the fresh eyes of a child. Look for what you can learn from them. And, enjoy a walk in the spiritual garden.

CHAPTER THREE

The Key to Life

11
Like My Brother Duane

*D*uane was my big brother. He was also my North Star, a guiding light, with no concern whether I would let his light help me find my own light, and my own way.

A couple of years older than me, he served as my bellwether. At age eight, he introduced me, a six-year-old, to after-school radio programs, which, until then, were only so much noise to me. He explained the story lines. He told the names of characters and their roles. The hero and his friends were on every week, their voices clear and determined, and they were more than ready, too, to see justice served to all villains.

So why mention Duane? Simply because his expressions of creativity fueled mine too.

The Shariyat-Ki-Sugmad, Book Two, says of creativity: "The creative self in man is that through which the ECK forces work, and the destructive self in man is that through which the Kal forces work."

Duane was therefore one of my early teachers in showing the power of stories. They bring subjects to life. Today, they are at the core of the ECK teachings, which the ECK, Holy Spirit, sees fit to have me pass along to you.

Duane, my big brother, was also my North Star, a guiding light. His expressions of creativity fueled mine too.

49

My brother also taught me to love pretty things.

One such instance that comes to me is a coloring contest he entered around age ten. The two prior years, no prize. But he tried again. This was a Christmas contest that the newspaper featured each year, with a cash prize for the top three winners. Duane chose bright colors and stayed within the lines.

So now, we also try to make ECK publications attractive.

Soon after the contest had ended, the mailman delivered a letter addressed to Duane. It said he had won third place. He could come anytime and pick up his cash prize.

Duane never gave up. Never. Once he set his mind to reaching some goal, he used every spark of creativity to reach it.

The whole family was so very proud of him. But, in a way, once it happened, I was not that surprised. He never gave up. Never. Once he set his mind to reaching some goal, he used every spark of creativity to reach it.

Walt Disney, American film producer, said, "If you can dream it, you can do it."

Henry David Thoreau, writer, adds a qualifying footnote to that. "If one advances confidently in the direction of his dreams," he said, "and endeavors to live the life which he has imagined, he will meet with a success unexpected in common hours."

About the time of the coloring contest, Duane got caught up by the model-airplane bug. He, at first, bought mainly plastic models, but he carefully applied the supplied decals onto the wings and body. Soon, however, he wanted flying models. No ready-to-fly planes were yet available, so a modeler was required to build his own from a kit. The balsa-wood pieces were printed with parts, like formers and struts, all coded with numbers and letters.

The whole puzzle needed to be fit together—pins and glue, silkspan and paint. It took a great deal of creativity and persistence to do the entire project right.

Duane's proudest achievement was a single-engined model with a four-foot wingspan. It gave him, me, and my other siblings many happy memories of summer fun.

Model planes led to his desire to fly the real thing. So he began to save money for lessons. That was money hard won. Helping neighbors thresh grain and bale hay brought in some money in summer. But in winter? Usually, there was no work.

One winter, however, at age sixteen, he got a lucky break. It was an *unlucky* break for a neighbor, whose arm was broken by a kick from a touchy cow.

Mornings and nights, Duane drove to Gerhard's place to milk his herd, which had nearly all "kickers," cows routinely beaten to make them behave. Duane was no pilgrim when it came to milking kickers. Our herd was full of them. Dad was of the same school as was Gerhard: beat them, and they will obey. But the cows never did.

With money in hand, Duane went to an airport and began flying lessons. He flew until the money ran out. Then, he scrambled to earn more of it.

Finally, finally, he made his solo flight.

He, soon after, qualified for a private pilot's license, then a commercial rating. The air force rejected him as a pilot—too short—but it put him in air traffic control. He ended up in a control tower at the busiest airport then in the United States. That experience helped him immensely

Finally, finally, he made his solo flight. He, soon after, qualified for a private pilot's license, then a commercial rating.

after service, when he got a job flying the planes of a regional carrier.

The point is, my brother followed his dreams. From him, I learned to follow mine.

So when I later found Eckankar, I "locked on" to it, heart and Soul, like a fighter plane's radar locks onto a target.

Let your own goal be God Consciousness. Never give up. Never!

Let your own goal be God Consciousness. Never give up. Never!

12

In the Spiritual Garden

*T*here is a popular garden show I catch early Saturday mornings. The host is a master gardener. He draws a large audience because he is knowledgeable, genial, and humble. He knows plants.

Yet for all that, he would be the first to admit to the limits of his learning, that there is still far more to learn about plants, even the ones in his own community or state. So you can well imagine that plant lovers of all levels of experience make sure to tune in to his weekly program, from horticulturalists at major universities to average people in small towns.

He welcomes all calls and emails. However, some beginners admit to being cowed by calls from highly informed gardeners.

This morning, for example, a woman who just loves tomatoes checked in to share her methods for growing them, both indoors and outdoors. The next caller, truly abashed, said, "I only want to ask about pruning my climbing roses."

The host quickly stepped in to restore her confidence.

He told her of the importance of her question, because other listeners could profit from it. A neo-

The garden-show caller said, "I only want to ask about pruning my climbing roses." The host quickly stepped in to restore her confidence.

phyte gardener might harbor the same question. Airing his answer to her would also let others add their experiences, which could lead to information he had not known.

It takes a big individual to make himself open to correction, or to give others credit for their input. He readily does both.

So you can see that the show's host is a very humble man.

* * *

Now, take a look at the stories on the ECKANKAR Blog or in the *Eckankar Journal*. They really are the journals of ordinary people like you, offering their stories for the enrichment of others. No two stories are alike. They range from spiritual lessons and insights to past lives and dreams. From meetings with ECK Masters to protection of the ECK (Holy Spirit), and more.

These ECK journalists include both newcomers and long-termers. The stories of all can be important to you.

These ECK journalists are like the gardeners who call the garden show mentioned above to share their experiences.

The ECKists include people who have been members of Eckankar for various lengths of time, including both newcomers and long-termers. The stories of all can be important to you. That is, assuming you are sincere in finding the most *direct* route home to God. How sincere are you?

In a real sense, ECK initiates depart from a comparison with gardeners for the simple reason that in the spiritual garden of ECK it often happens that hard-learned lessons are forgotten.

Yes, forgotten!

I know persons who once could boast of the most fantastic dream and everyday experiences, when their humility was great and their faith in the Mahanta, the Inner Master, was rock steady.

Since those heady days of being in the flow of Divine Spirit, something terrible has happened to them. They have grown pumpkin heads. They had taken the Master's guidance for granted. So, eventually, they lost it. It all happened so gradually, though, that now they imagine they have become "masters in their own right." It is a catchphrase with them.

Please, do not let that happen to you. Read ECK stories with the fresh eyes of a child. Look for what you can learn from them.

And, enjoy a walk in the spiritual garden.

Enjoy a walk in the spiritual garden.

13

What about the Expressions of Consciousness?

"This world offers such a rich and varied realm of consciousness," I told friends, "that it's a joy and privilege to be alive." Our instincts, however, often provoke us to ridicule ideas and behaviors offensive to us but really harmful to no one at all.

Expressions of consciousness too unlike our own raise our ire.

But all expressions of it are necessary in the grand scheme of creation.

Jean de La Fontaine, of seventeenth-century France, was an absentminded dreamer. Stories about him attest to that. Well liked but unreliable in love or business, he nonetheless had a poetic genius for creating fables. A French ECKist once sent me his *Selected Fables*. She assured me that all children have learned the fables of Jean de La Fontaine.

"A good start for a spiritual life," she added.

So let's consider "The Acorn and the Pumpkin" as an example of a good start.

This world offers such a rich and varied realm of consciousness that it's a joy and privilege to be alive.

A country bumpkin was studying a pumpkin. "What was the Creator thinking?"

A country bumpkin was studying a pumpkin. Its huge girth and thin vine made him exclaim, "What was the Creator thinking, putting it on the ground? A noble food like that would have been better placed in a mighty oak."

God got this wrong, he thought. *A mix-up, certainly.*

The acorn would have better matched the pumpkin's slender vine, he mused. *How could God have made such a witless blunder?* This puzzle taxed his vacuous mind and offered him no peace.

Soon he went off to rest under a great oak tree.

A falling acorn assaulted his tender nose, jarring him awake. "Oh, I'm bleeding!" he cried.

This incident expanded our philosopher's mind. *What luck it wasn't heavier*, he thought. *Suppose the acorn had been a pumpkin. Yes, the Creator did get it exactly right.*

The man went home that night praising God for all things under the heavens.

A silly tale? Not in the least. It illustrates the spiritual principle that everything has its place. The way the acorn and pumpkin happen to grow is part of the grand scheme. Even the simpleton, who demonstrates a change in consciousness at the end, is by then left with a fuller understanding of the divine order.

The following story is of "Ailsa," her husband, and their cat. It shows the infectious nature of happiness.

One morning, Ailsa determined to be especially happy. A moment of pure joy ran through her. The cat immediately felt it too and displayed an unrestrained and enthusiastic side-to-side rolling on a small rug. His performance lasted much longer than usual.

A third Soul there, besides Ailsa and the cat, was her husband. Observing the feline's antics, he exclaimed, "The cat's not been like that for a long time!"

Happiness shows.

Ailsa tells of a second incident many would term decidedly unusual. Yet it easily fits within the spacious boundaries of the many expressions of consciousness among us.

She talks with birds and plants.

An unusual gift, she is the first to admit. "Of course," she says, "I am used to animals and plants talking, but always amazed."

Their desires may seem of little importance, easy to brush aside.

Ailsa parked her car outside the local food market. A lot of snow covered the ground. On the store's roof she spotted a lone blackbird. She studied it; it studied her. Then it took a nosedive straight at her, and when closest to her, it said, "Get me an apple!"

A lone black-bird took a nosedive straight at Ailsa and said, "Get me an apple!"

"Of course," she replied, startled. Some birds are so flighty.

Ailsa finished shopping. As she stepped from the store and headed for her car, the bird swooped again.

"You forgot the apple!"

She headed back inside, selected a big prize apple, and was about to set it on some boards outside where it could be seen. But where was the bird? "Here it is now!" she called out. The bird was alongside her as soon as she let go of the apple.

Before she even got into her car, the blackbird had dragged the apple into the snow and was

Now, let's look carefully at the verbal and visual expressions of others that raise our hackles. Are those expressions really harmful to someone?

happily pecking away at it.

Ailsa reckoned this a "lovely experience."

Her stories are two small examples of the countless expressions of consciousness amid the panoply of creation. Of them, she writes, "I hope I didn't sound bigheaded when saying I am used to animals and plants talking. I can only bow to their love and wisdom."

Now, let's look carefully at the verbal and visual expressions of others that raise our hackles. Are those expressions *really* harmful to someone?

If not, let them go. We'll be better off spiritually for it in the end.

14
A Few Good Stories
from You

$\mathcal{H}$ere is a medley of your stories. A unifying thread tying these stories into a single narrative is Soul's great love for God.

Let's see how that plays out.

"Titine" was still living in Africa when her older brother translated, died. She'd loved him greatly. He had been about to receive his Second Initiation at the time of his demise. She'd been at his deathbed. In deep emotional pain, she'd sobbed, "I will come back for you, if necessary, because we are not done after this life."

She didn't understand the implications of that vow.

Three years later, Titine's oldest daughter, also dear to the brother, became pregnant. Six months along, Titine's brother came to her in a dream. He said he was coming back now because he knew she'd not return to earth.

Two weeks before his birth, he came to her daughter, telling her of his intentions.

Mother and daughter told no one of his plan.

Titine assisted at the delivery and witnessed

an extraordinary moment. "I saw Soul integrate with the body at the very moment of birth."

An exceptional event, to be sure.

In roughly the same time frame, a cousin told her of a beloved aunt in Benin, lying in a coma. Doctors expected her death in the next few hours. It was important for Titine to visit her immediately.

At the clinic, relatives guided her to the sickroom. Many priests and nuns were in the room, because her aunt was a devout Catholic.

Titine sat down by her aunt's side.

The moment she did, her aunt came to. The sick woman screamed repeatedly, "Who are those people with you?" Her daughter tried to calm her. "It's just Titine." She couldn't see the people.

"I know this is Titine," the old woman shot back, "but she's brought other people with her!" Titine knew her aunt could see the ECK Masters she'd asked to accompany her. Then her aunt slipped into a coma again.

The narrowed eyes of the priests and nuns now watched Titine intently.

Her aunt soon awoke, shrieking the same words as earlier. Titine drew a chair near and held the old lady's hand. Everyone in the room observed the least of these movements. The aunt then became comatose.

Titine was happy to know the ECK Masters were really with her.

The day after, her aunt regained consciousness. She wanted to see Titine. But once bitten, twice shy. Titine had a strong reluctance to return for a second drubbing.

Three days passed.

"I saw Soul integrate with the body at the very moment of birth." An exceptional event, to be sure.

Her aunt told the doctors she'd refuse any treatments as long as she didn't see her niece. She thought someone was keeping her away.

Titine ran to meet her. Her aunt said, "The only treatment I want is from those persons who came with you. It's because of them I'm still alive." She added, "They treated and cured me." Titine confirmed that the doctors hadn't altered their treatments.

Titine's aunt said, "It's because of those persons who came with you I'm still alive."

Her aunt identified some of the ECK Masters from photos Titine showed her.

The old woman survived another six months. But she requested that Titine supervise her funeral, a great honor.

Titine, in a closing note, said, "The whole experience gave me many opportunities to share the HU."

I'm overjoyed to welcome "Bob" back to Eckankar. His story is of a man's spiritual journey since he first came across the ECK teachings some thirty years ago. He'd studied four series of ECK discourses.

Five years later, a new job at the San Diego Wild Animal Park, training elephants, led him to take a rest from his ECK pursuits. He listed two reasons. First, the Inner Master advised it, and second, his own sensibilities agreed. He needed to keep his feet planted on the ground.

What's more, his mind needed to be fully alert while walking among a herd of elephants.

He also thought it smart to slow down his karma in light of the present danger.

Three years later, he planned to marry. His fiancée asked that he place his ECK books in storage. Her family, Southern Baptists, was visiting to attend their wedding. Moreover, her father, head of the deacons, would frown upon Eckankar.

Two decades later, the couple traveled to Alabama for the funeral of her mother. A falling-out took place with her family.

They returned home. His wife announced she wanted to learn about Eckankar. Bob retrieved the ECK books from storage, which they began to study together. His wife has taken to Eckankar. She's read nearly all the Master's books.

Bob waited for his wife to finish her karmic obligations so they might travel home to God together.

These stories show the power of love.

Love is the key to life.

These stories show the power of love. Love is the key to life.

Divine love is the sun in Walter's life. It can, and should be, in yours too.

CHAPTER FOUR

A World of Gifts

15
Gifts of Love

"Jim" was in charge of directing helpers to load trailers after a major ECK seminar. Due to good planning and willing hands, the group finished two hours before the driver was to arrive.

The volunteers and ECK staff who had elected to stay sang a closing HU song. It was to thank the Mahanta for the many gifts of love they had received over the weekend.

Jim realized that the HU song in itself was a gift of love.

The day was wearing on. And with it, the temperature began to drop. There was no reason for the others to stay longer, so Jim thanked them and let them go.

Two hours to wait!

With a lull in activity, Jim suddenly realized he felt cold and hungry. Nothing to do but tough it out, he thought.

But the Mahanta had a few surprises in store for him—gifts of love.

He took a final look around the dock area to be sure nothing had been overlooked. He also scanned the stage area. On a table near the stage, two gifts awaited him: a knit hat that matched

Nothing to do but tough it out, Jim thought. But the Mahanta had a few surprises in store for him—gifts of love.

the color of his jacket, and a piece of chocolate cake on a plate—complete with a fork too.

Jim, of course, tore into the cake. Then he put on the cap and returned to the loading area to await the truck.

His heart was full of love for these welcome gifts from the Mahanta.

Then, yet another gift!

There was a small folding chair nestled behind a large dock post. So Jim sat on the dock, enjoying the warming sunshine that poured through the clouds. The Mahanta sure was thoughtful. Jim reflected upon all the love and blessings of the past few days.

A nudge compelled him to glance over to his left. Were his eyes playing tricks on him?

Earlier, an ECK staff member had offered the others two granola bars, but no one had taken them. Well, Jim did the natural thing and gratefully accepted the Master's gifts of never-ending love.

The truck driver arrived soon after and hauled the trailers away.

More was to come. The Mahanta also gave Jim a gift of spiritual understanding.

Yet more was to come. The Mahanta also gave Jim a gift of spiritual understanding. During the ECK seminar, he had felt such love for the Master that he had offered to take on a part of his spiritual burden. But things took a quite unexpected turn.

The trailers had to be unloaded the following day, and Jim hurt his back while doing it. He learned that only the Mahanta has the spiritual strength for such an enormous task as to shoulder the Mahanta's responsibilities.

That lesson was a gift in itself.

Now, let's turn to "Kay," for she also received gifts of love.

She holds the position of curator of collections at a history museum. One day, as she and Jill, her intern, were packing up long-forgotten items to move them to a new warehouse, they came upon what looked like a stick of dynamite.

Jill had run into a similar situation at another museum. She knew the great danger it posed.

"Don't touch it!" she warned. "Dynamite becomes more unstable and volatile with time."

Kay, however, wasn't sure it actually was dynamite. Just at that moment, movers delivered more packing boxes, and one of them confirmed that it really was dynamite. So Kay called the police bomb squad, and soon an officer came to take it away for safe disposal.

The Mahanta's protection was certainly a gift of love.

But what did the experience mean?

The next morning in contemplation, Kay was told by the Master to treat the experience like a dream. So she wrote it down as one.

She was at work, clearing off the top shelf of some storage units. Kay knew she had a lot to do, so she got right to it. The objects on the top shelf were karma. She was up to moving them, and fast.

The dynamite was old, forgotten anger. It had to go.

The movers helped her identify the dynamite. The huge moving project at the museum is to help her quickly move through a lot of karma.

Mike, the officer, didn't want her to call him sir, but Mike. "Sir" is like "Sri" to Kate. Thus, "Sri Mike" easily transforms into "Mahanta" for her.

The Mahanta's protection was certainly a gift of love. But what did the experience mean?

The Mahanta is the only one who can safely remove her anger so it won't blow up her world. Thus, two gifts of love: protection from harm, and help with removing old karma.

Both Jim and Kay are grateful for the Master's gifts of love.

16
These Simple Miracles

"Jahzara" is a Nigerian woman who wished to attend an upcoming ECK Worldwide Seminar but couldn't. So during the seminar she put her full attention there. Happily, her nighttime dreams were in 3-D, finding her with ECK friends doing things together.

In one dream someone reminded her to always sing *HU* in all she did, no matter how minor the thing might be. Still another dream found her in a lecture room. All she could remember from the lecturer was a single phrase: "These simple miracles."

*   *   *

And then it was Sunday, October 22, the beginning of the new spiritual year of Eckankar. But contrarily, it also appeared to mark a rough start in the year for her.

She and her son had been out running errands. He was at the wheel. Whatever the nature of the "experience" that landed them in the police station is unclear, but the incident certainly did raise her dander.

In any event, she knew her son was innocent of the petty charge laid against him.

Whatever the nature of the "experience" that landed Jahzara and her son in the police station is unclear, but the incident certainly did raise her dander.

Remembering the Master's promise of always being with her, she started to sing *HU* silently. A thought slipped across her mind: Was there something the ECK wanted her to learn?

Then, a very strong nudge.

Jahzara placed a call to her special friend, the Mahanta. "Please take charge of this case," she said into her phone.

Since none of her friends had responded to her calls, she carried her phone into a corner of the room and placed a call to her special friend, the Mahanta. Onlookers would guess it was just an ordinary call.

"Please take charge of this case," she said into her phone.

At that very moment, a police officer entered the waiting room. "Madam," he declared, "when things like this happen in your life, it offers an opportunity for you to thank God, because you don't know what might otherwise have happened. But God used this to delay you."

When he'd finished, she thanked him and said, "That's one of the things we learn in our religion, Eckankar."

"So you belong to the HU family!"

She affirmed it while also noting that today was the ECK Spiritual New Year. After a friendly exchange, the police officer said she and her son were free to go. To her son, Jahzara later remarked, "Can you see the Mahanta's love in action?" Both were greatly relieved and happy with the outcome.

Now, would you like to drop in on "Thea"?

Filled with love, she determined to give a gift to her ECK Temple, a framed picture of the Master. But how often doesn't life crimp our plans? Paying for the photo and having it framed would be anything but easy, since she'd not received back pay from her job in nearly five months. That did present a hurdle.

In the meantime, she'd received a small sum of welfare for sustenance, but it was hardly enough to obtain the picture. And there was no hope at all of receiving a few months' back pay. In spite of everything, she was set on seeing the Master's picture in the temple by Sunday, October 22. It was now Friday.

Looking for a solution, she asked the Master if it was OK to borrow money and fulfill her pledge. No answer was forthcoming.

After the HU Song Friday evening, she returned home to catch up on chores. She checked her messages and was stunned to learn of a credit alert issued by her bank. She had money coming. The credit was very nearly what was needed to obtain the photo.

The impossible was suddenly within reach.

The impossible was suddenly within reach.

And indeed, the Master's photo did grace its assigned place before the ECK Temple's first event on Sunday, October 22.

Thea reported a second instance of the Master's love and help. A few minutes before the end of work one day, she'd felt a strong urge to begin singing *HU*. She did so and kept it up even on her walk to visit a friend.

Then it happened!

She'd been walking alongside a road that crossed a major intersection. Suddenly, a car's squealing tires broke the calm. A runaway car, whose brakes had failed, came to rest mere inches from her. The car had nearly struck her. A very close call.

This experience reassured her of the Master's love and protection. And singing *HU* had provided the shield to safeguard her from injury. The lesson? It was vital to do the Spiritual Exercises of ECK. In fact, one must even *be* the HU.

Thea knows that God's love is absolutely with and within her. All she needs to do is open her heart to it.

So how else has divine love come to light her life? She related a yet-to-be-resolved puzzle. Nearing the end of her childbearing years, she remains childless. It troubles her. She dearly wants a child.

It happened that she was spending the night with a suitor. In the beginning of their relationship, he had seemed aloof and distant, but since then he was showing a warm and affectionate side. She loved him and would gladly be his wife. Yet that very night with him there came a troubling dream that suggested he would, in the end, leave her empty and unfulfilled.

Will this dream prove to be one of those simple miracles?

Meanwhile, she is simply surrendering her heart to the Mahanta. She'll go slow with this relationship until the will of God clearly prevails.

Will this dream prove to be one of those simple miracles? Time tells all. Some answers just don't come easy.

17
Gifts, Gifts, and More Gifts

*O*nce, on the inner planes, a jolly wit with carrot-colored hair eyed a fellow and commented on an ill-advised action by the other. "I know you wished it to be so," he said, "but where was your wishful *thinking*?"

In other words, the other had done something without regard for consequences. And they had cost him dearly.

That's how karma comes about.

"Connie," a chela for many years, had an important realization. She suddenly saw that she alone was responsible for the way her life was. Everything in it was of her own making.

"Good, bad, pretty, ugly—it's all of my own making," she confessed.

What an important insight! She had, of course, known this basic ECK principle for years, but now, she acknowledged, she was beginning to understand it at a greater level. In addition, she saw why it was so important to stop making more negative karma. She realized that continuing to do so was, in a real sense, standing in her own way.

Connie suddenly saw that she alone was responsible for the way her life was.

The Mahanta, the Living ECK Master bestows a priceless gift upon all ECK chelas. He shows them the importance of every thought, word, and deed. Also, to avoid making more negative karma, the importance of doing everything in the name of the Sugmad, the ECK, and the Mahanta. And, too, Thy will, not mine, be done.

You surely have heard these things and know them by heart. May I suggest, however, that on occasion you make them the subject of a contemplation.

Connie had one more insight. She had been reading an ECK discourse on how the Master removes karma in the dream state. She got an image of falling on her face and hurting herself while biking. So that was the reason she was forgetting her dreams, in which the Master was lifting some of her karma, she supposed; some bike falls and injuries she need not remember.

The Master's whole life is given over to you, to help you to someday stand on your own spiritual feet.

That is the way the Master works. His whole life is given over to you, to help you to someday stand on your own spiritual feet.

It is a gift freely given.

A new member of Eckankar said that one thing in the ECK teachings had made her jump up and down. It was where she learned there is no such thing as a coincidence in life. Everything coming into one's life simply marks the return of something the individual had once set into motion.

This ECKist added that Eckankar is also "the only place I've ever seen . . . where they meant it."

Another woman had been through a number of religions. From the sum of their teachings, she concluded that "God is an angry God." Her conviction arose because they were always saying, "Do this!" "Don't do that!" She said it was no fun; it was boring. It drove her to becoming a cynic, suspicious of all human behavior.

Then she found Eckankar on the internet. She requested a free book and suspended her cynicism long enough to find its contents interesting.

One thing led to another. She went to the ECK Center in town for a year without joining. She never stayed for refreshments after the ECK discussion class to talk. She said, "I got in and got out."

Gradually, a discovery finally sank in: God is not mean, cruel, or punishing. Then she became an ECKist.

Gradually, a discovery finally sank in: God is not mean, cruel, or punishing. Then she became an ECKist.

Not only does the Master help chelas with their karma, or help them see basic ECK principles as being key players in their spiritual lives, he also helps them find Eckankar in the first place.

This was the experience of "Gino," a young Italian. At around the age of twenty, he joined a meditation class and saw the Mahanta in his meditations. (Gino did not know then it was the Mahanta. It would be five years before he found ECK.)

Soon, he began researching other paths.

A couple of people Gino knew were ECKists, but he did not know that. One day, within earshot of Gino, they began to talk about the Mahanta and Eckankar. He listened to them about a minute. In the space of those few seconds, he knew he wanted to become a member. The next day, he did.

Having seen the Mahanta five years before he found ECK, Gino knows the Mahanta had chosen him. Gino had not chosen anything.

What reasons do others give for becoming ECK chelas?

"Constance" knew about the ECK teachings for several years before they clicked for her. The scriptures of other religions just were not the ticket. They did not give her the feeling she could take charge of her own spirituality, but the ECK teachings did.

The Master gives you and all others generous gifts, and many more gifts too.

So the Master gives you and all others generous gifts as detailed in the stories above, and many more gifts too.

Gifts, gifts, and even more gifts besides.

18
Help on the Spot

"Paul" is a Nigerian born into an ECK family. So he enjoyed all the spiritual aids that made his life easy.

Around fourteen, he left home for a boarding school which only allowed prayers to be done the Christian or the Muslim way. Paul, of course, was careful not to let his beliefs in ECK become known to the faculty.

Some way or another, a Christian teacher discovered Paul's secret during the third year of secondary school, when Paul was sixteen or seventeen. The teacher called Paul into his office. He preached to Paul. The two argued at length, until the youth finally gave in. The two prayed in a Christian way; then his teacher blessed him.

Paul was relieved to now be a Christian, since he and his brother had been the two lone ECKists in the hostel. He could, as a Christian, pray with his friends. Paul finally felt he belonged at the school. And life went on.

One night he had a dream while sleeping in the hostel. There was a volcano eruption in the school; liquid lights were falling from the sky, burning things and people.

One night Paul had a dream while sleeping in the hostel. There was a volcano eruption in the school.

Paul began to run to escape the disaster.

Looking back, he noticed a red Indian with a long, sharp knife in hot pursuit. He ran until unable to flee any longer. Then, remembering he was a Christian, he screamed, "Jesus!"

That quickly, the Indian disappeared. Paul woke up happy.

But two weeks later, the dream was back! Same red Indian, same sharp knife, same terror. Paul was confused. Had not his pursuer been defeated?

Fortunately, he remembered Eckankar. He screamed, "Mahanta!" The Master responded on the spot.

This time, the Indian did not vanish as before, but something wonderful now took place: the man dropped his knife. There was so much love in his eyes. He apologized profusely to Paul for having given him such a fright. They made up and parted ways.

The dream never troubled Paul again.

Love, he realized, mattered above all things.

Five years later, he finally learned the dream's meaning. Love, he realized, was all around him. Love mattered above all things. It was in humans, animals, religions, and the like.

But Eckankar, he realized, has so much *divine love*, waiting to be realized, tapped, and shared.

Paul is still in ECK today.

In this next story, "John" sees how the Mahanta, the Inner Master, helps in both the little and big things of life.

John had a feeling one night of stagnating on a spiritual plateau. He sang *HU* and surrendered the negative feeling. That very night, a dream saw him teaching many people in a large classroom.

Then, a second dream.

Somebody (the Inner Master) brought John's eyeglasses. "Look," the Master said, "one of the temple pieces will soon fall off because its screw is loose! It'll be hard to find so small a screw if it falls off."

When John got up, he merely lifted his glasses from the table, when the screw fell safely onto the table; he fixed the screw.

Further, two weeks later, he was asked to teach an ECK class. This occurred after being passed over as a teacher due to new, greater responsibilities in other ECK duties. John knows personally that the Mahanta helps in all matters, great and small.

The Mahanta helps in all matters, great and small.

Both John and Paul learned that the Master can, when necessary, give help right on the spot.

19
The Sun of God's Love in Their Lives

"Walter" had been reflecting upon the question Why are you still in ECK?

After weighing a number of possibilities, he decided the main reason was "to maintain that direct linkup with Divine Spirit—for divine love." But that is hard to say in public. So he finds it easier to speak of spiritual freedom or total awareness.

Choices in Walter's runner-up list include

- The protection of the Mahanta—such as three near-collisions so far in this life (maybe even more unnoticed ones)
- The freedom to choose where to go or what to consider during a Spiritual Exercise of ECK
- Dream travel and working off karma in the dream state
- Intuition and nudges that never fail
- A chance to realize God

All these benefits are spin-offs from Walter's direct linkup with Divine Spirit, the ECK—the source of divine love.

All these benefits are spin-offs from his direct linkup with Divine Spirit, the ECK—the source of divine love.

Divine love is the sun in Walter's life. It can, and should be, in yours too.

Divine love can work miracles for you, if you let it. Walter testifies to that.

Another who has implicit faith in the ways of the Holy Spirit is "Alberto," a citizen of Mexico. He and his son were flying to Minneapolis. Alberto was going on business; his son, returning to college after a school holiday.

The first leg of their flight, to Dallas, went smoothly. Father and son genuinely enjoyed each other's company.

They went through immigration, picked up their luggage, then headed for customs. Alberto suddenly felt apprehension. They had just surrendered their luggage for loading onto the second flight. Alberto looked back. Everything seemed in order, so they walked away.

Yet a gnawing unease remained.

In Minneapolis, his son paced around the luggage carousel. In the meantime, Alberto sang *HU* quietly to himself. It is something he often does while waiting, because it helps him release tension, while also opening his heart to the divine love that is always there, for the accepting.

To his surprise, Alberto felt completely calm. No impatience. No indignation. No badgering the agent with questions.

After the last piece of luggage was removed and the carousel stopped, father and son knew they had a problem. Their bags were lost.

An airline representative took their contact information. To his surprise, Alberto felt completely calm, very matter-of-fact about the situation. No impatience. No indignation. No badgering the agent with questions.

Alberto just knew everything *was* in the right place. All he could do was trust the ECK.

That night he went to bed, listening to a talk by the Living ECK Master, "A Golden Contract." He drifted off to sleep with this truth in mind: "Every encounter, without exception, is there to move Soul along spiritually on Its way home to God. That's every encounter, every event, without exception."

Early next morning, a caller said the bags had arrived and would soon be delivered.

Now came a surprise!

The deliveryman was an ECK High Initiate, a friend. This was not his regular job, but he was merely filling in for a friend.

"What are the chances? One in a billion!" he exclaimed to Alberto.

In a letter to the Living ECK Master, Alberto said, "You are the sun in my life."

He wondered that the Mahanta had sent an emissary—a brother in ECK—to deliver a gift of love. The only thing that could have surprised him more that morning would have been to see the Master in person, standing on that sidewalk!

Maybe another time.

In a letter to the Living ECK Master, Alberto said, "You are the sun in my life."

"Daddy, what did the ECK Masters do to become the ECK Masters?"

CHAPTER FIVE

Turning a New Leaf

20
Helping the ECK
Is Helping Yourself

long time ago, in another life, "Abbie" was assistant to the village medical guru. Abbie was a bit lazy. It was hard work helping to go out into the hills and countryside to gather herbs. What she loathed even more was having to grind them, pound them, decoct them. All necessary to turn them into healing potions.

The villagers depended upon the healer's prescriptions to cool their fevers, mend broken bones, become fertile, soothe tooth- and earaches, and ease many other ills too.

But Abbie was lazy and selfish. Who would ever know that some remedies she prepared were watered down? The healer trusted her. So she got away with this chicanery during those long-gone days, but the effects have stalked her into the present, where they manifest in many ills and discomforts. In short, she suffers from poor health.

ECK Master Rebazar Tarzs had pulled up this former lifetime so Abbie could learn the reason for many of her current challenges.

As you can imagine, she had to take a hard

ECK Master Rebazar Tarzs had pulled up this former lifetime so Abbie could learn the reason for many of her current challenges.

91

look at herself. She found that selfishness and vanity still lurked far beneath the skin, mental passions that she had imagined were long gone. It would take awhile to absorb this unnerving insight.

Eternally upbeat in outlook, Abbie looks upon herself and her ancient crimes as being repairable, to a great extent.

However, she also knows that many of those effects are hard-wired into her genetic code and will take a lot of patience to resolve. Rebazar had revealed that past life to her because Abbie was now at a point in spiritual unfoldment where she could address those old shortcomings and do something about them. And so she is.

With the aid of health practitioners, she is tackling her health concerns, with an eye to remodeling herself. Many of these concerns will be lessened to a very large degree.

Abbie's insight: "Soul can turn a new leaf, even if the body is permanently wired. So that's my goal."

Her insight: "Soul can turn a new leaf, even if the body is permanently wired. So that's my goal."

Abbie has learned the importance of giving to the Holy Spirit, the ECK, with her whole heart, body, and mind. She is on a Vahana team, speaks at ECK services, and participates in other area ECK events. She is serving the ECK not out of selfishness, but out of love.

And so she is helping herself too.

"Jodie" shared reflections of the past month, for she, like Abbie, learned once again that serving the ECK helps oneself spiritually.

She had had recurring fears of being a failure, that she was not serving the Mahanta enough. She had to let go of those fears. After much contemplation on the situation, she says, much love flowed through her like a river.

The voice of the Mahanta spoke in the stillness: "Discipline, Jodie! Do one small thing at a time, and do it with love, for love and love alone."

Jodie, like Abbie, was grateful for the chance to examine her weakness and check her ego.

She reflected, too, upon her RESA's comment: "Mahanta, make me a greater vehicle to serve Sugmad, the ECK, and you." The RESA had felt the same fear as Jodie, of not serving the Mahanta fully. Jodie then realized what she had again forgotten—it is all about being love and giving love.

Around that time, "Eve," a dear friend of hers, called. Could she catch a ride with Jodie and her husband, "Alain," to the weekly writers group they all attended? The couple talked it over and readily agreed. Alain called Eve back while Jodie changed clothes; then they fixed a quick meal and jumped into the car. They needed to leave as soon as possible to be on time for the meeting, since it was a snowy winter night.

On the drive, the three chatted about the weather and other happenings. Jodie felt the energy shift. The Master's love was strong, flowing among them.

The meeting went well. Then they took Eve home, and she said, "You have no idea how much sharing the ride and the company mean to me." During the ride, she had told of how challenging her life had recently been. The ride with Jodie and Alain was just the reassurance she had needed of the Mahanta's love for her.

Jodie's heart melted. She had received a gift as well. It was the awareness to remind herself that no matter how small an act of kindness to

Jodie's gift was the awareness that no matter how small an act of kindness to another may be, it can have a profound effect.

another may be, it can have a profound effect.
An outpouring of divine love uplifts all.

21
Open Your Heart, Then Your Eyes and Ears

"*D*ee's" dream puzzled her. Nevertheless, she wrote it in her dream journal, a long-standing habit. As she logged it, the meaning became clear.

So what was her dream?

She had driven up to a large building, with an old metal folding chair in the bed of her truck. Many people were clustered along the long, winding sidewalk that led to the building's entrance. Some had stacks of chairs like Dee's. They waited patiently.

Dee pushed her single chair past them, knowing she could sit in it and rest, if she wanted to. But she did not.

Inside the churchlike building, she folded her chair and stood it along a nearby wall. Many thick, well-cushioned seats were available, with only a quarter or third of them occupied. Dee chose one near the front that provided a good view.

Then Dee awoke.

As she began to record her dream, its meaning slowly became clear. Here is what she learned:

Dee's dream puzzled her. As she began to record it, its meaning slowly became clear.

Her old metal folding chair, with its scratched paint, dents, and a want of padding, signified old ideas, fears, and hang-ups—all of which were holding her back from God. Her old chair, like those of others, showed that their owners were still relying on those worn-out ideas.

Dee could enter that temple because she had moved beyond her old state of consciousness. She had but one chair; the others still held on to many.

Anyway, Dee was able to fold hers and set it aside. The many open seats inside the building were a sharp reminder that the path of ECK is not immediately for all. The thick, padded seats inside held meaning too. They were like the love, guidance, and protection of the Mahanta.

They made life so much better than before ECK.

Dee learned from this dream. She had been open to the Mahanta, then watched and listened for whatever was to come.

"Vicky" also shared a dream. Years ago she had one, in which an epileptic cousin was a symbol for Vicky's stubbornness, which left her troubled upon awakening. Its meaning had always eluded her. Only years later would she prove able to comprehend the message so long hidden from her spiritual eyesight.

Recently, that all changed with the coming of a new dream. Now it all clicked.

Vicky's dream was of a snowstorm, which had downed power lines. She instructed others with her not to touch any wires. Her epileptic cousin did.

In the next scene, Vicky saw her cousin lying motionless on the snow, electrocuted. Workers took

The thick, padded seats were like the love, guidance, and protection of the Mahanta. They made life so much better than before ECK.

her remains away.

Vicky's early dream had been about her own refusal to surrender to the ECK. This refusal was like her cousin's stubbornness. It was an ugly aberration. The dream showed Vicky that she had finally won release from the claws of stubbornness. The whiteness of the snow was an indication of that.

So these two dreams tell of progress in Vicky's unfoldment over the years. The following story is hers too. But it shows her service to the Mahanta in ordinary and everyday affairs.

She is a teacher. Some weeks ago, she was called upon to be a substitute teacher for a gym class. However, when enough trained coaches showed up, she was free to sit in the bleachers and watch the proceedings.

Vicky soon saw trouble brewing on the floor.

A youth was harassing a less fortunate classmate. The former showed a real dislike for his victim, a malice which Vicky correctly guessed was due to past-life karma.

The main coach called the offender to task. He seemed to threaten him with severe discipline.

The boy was afraid of being expelled. He ended up seated on the sidelines, still bristling with anger. Vicky went over and sat beside him. As he spilled out his anger for his classmate, she told him of a humming sound, scientifically proven to help one calm down.

As the boy spilled out his anger for his classmate, Vicky told him of a humming sound, scientifically proven to help one calm down.

He was doubtful. Never had he heard of it. Moreover, he was too angry to even try it.

So Vicky hummed *HU* for a while, then sang it for him. Soon after, she got up and left. He later came up and said he had tried it; it actually worked! Then he left to board the bus, which he had been afraid to do because of his rage.

It pays spiritually to open your heart, then your eyes and ears too.

A few weeks later, she had him in another class. Humor and life sparkled in his eyes. Yet he remained disciplined in the midst of unruly kids.

*   *   *

Whether we are talking about the inner or outer life, it pays spiritually to open your heart, then your eyes and ears too.

22
Anger and Arrogance Meet Humility

Sage and humorist Mark Twain observed, "Good breeding consists in concealing how much we think of ourselves and how little we think of the other person."

What an apt definition for faked humility. But rest assured that the Mahanta will undress such conceits and expose them for what they are. Yet he does more. Along with them, he also catches up one's impatience, anger, and vanity. A well-rounded service, don't you think?

"James" confides that he was on the outs about something with his wife. He walked into his room and sat down on the edge of the bed, feeling bad. *What had set this off? How can I make it better?* Just then, the door opened and his six-year-old son came in, with a question on his mind.

"Daddy, what did the ECK Masters do to become the ECK Masters?"

His question caught James off guard. But it also struck him how wonderfully the Master spoke to his heart and nudged him back on a spiritual track.

He realized that one of the things the ECK Masters did to become ECK Masters was to remain balanced in all circumstances, no matter what happened. The Master had spoken through his son.

James took immediate action.

He changed his attitude and his feelings on the spot. Above all, he removed his attention from the situation and placed it upon the Inner Master. Only moments later, he became happier and relaxed.

This incident served as a reminder. He would listen to every conversation with a more open heart, to hear the voice of the Master.

"Mark," like James, is sincere about doing things right. He likes to tell friends in a humorous way, "Eckankar is not a part-time business. It is not something you practice only on Sundays. It is a full-time job."

Fortunately, Mark can appreciate the light side of things.

He tells of an occasion when he asked in contemplation, "Please, Mahanta, make me a channel for the love of God." He contemplated awhile on his request. Then, when the opportunity came, he nearly missed it.

Sent on some assignment to his city's university campus, he was approached by an unknown gentleman. Mark was in no mood for any interference. His attention was on his assignment.

Then the inner communication lines opened.

"I thought you wanted to be a channel for the love of God," said the Master.

Mark checked himself, but even then, with some impatience.

The other person explained his difficulty in

Mark asked, "Please, Mahanta, make me a channel for the love of God." Then, when the opportunity came, he nearly missed it.

choosing the best combination of subjects to pursue at the university. He added that he felt that Mark was the right person to help him deal with this issue. Mark realized that he was indeed well placed to help him.

After discussing the career the man wanted to pursue, they quickly resolved the matter to his satisfaction.

And Mark also was the happier for serving as a channel for the Master, and more humble for the privilege.

Mark woke one morning with the word "humility" on his lips. Did he still have to pay attention to that? But the lesson was soon in coming.

Mark tells of another lesson. He woke one morning with the word "humility" on his lips. Did *he* still have to pay attention to that? Weren't impatience, anger, and vanity things of the past? This was quite an unexpected message.

But the lesson was soon in coming.

It so happened that he had to see his auto mechanic that day. The auto service facility was at the extreme end of other enterprises in a large area designated for such businesses.

Driving in from one of the two entrances was a much shorter approach.

When Mark had nearly reached his destination, he found a truck blocking the way. He studied the situation. Men were loading pipes onto the truck. He honked his horn for the driver to pull over so he could pass.

One of the workers shrugged him off. Mark could as well go back to the other entrance, that shrug suggested. But it was really too far now.

Mark fumed. Who was that guy to treat him like that? Such a display of unreasonableness was just too much!

Furious, he started to get out of his vehicle,

when the word "humility" flitted across his mind. So he ignored the undisciplined worker. Instead, he stopped in his tracks and asked for the one in charge, but in a more loving way.

Mark was humming *HU* now.

The man in charge appeared, and, without Mark having to say another word, had the driver move the truck.

The lesson, as Mark saw it:

Each of us is Soul, with the same potential for spiritual growth. Some recognize this earlier than others.

As we go up the spiritual ladder, there is the temptation to look down on those we think have not achieved our spiritual stature. However, each of us is Soul, with the same potential for spiritual growth. Some recognize this earlier than others.

Just as those ahead of us provide us with all the love and the encouragement we need to climb up, despite our several failings, so must we accord others seeking the "path" respect and understanding.

Beautifully said. Thank you, Mark.

23

"That's Irrelevant!"

The first real cold snap had hit Minnesota, winter's calling card. I was in a food store that has a loft with easy chairs and a few tables. Customers use this loft to relax, eat, play with their computers, or visit with friends.

A fiftyish woman was on her computer. Her graying blond hair was tied back severely; dark-rimmed glasses framed her owlish eyes, while the corners of her mouth turned down.

Barely looking up from the screen, she snapped toward me, "Would a dead car battery keep the doors from locking?"

What made her think I would know? I had been scanning books and magazines on a display rack near her.

How much did *she* know about auto maintenance? Two things were involved, though—a dead battery and a door that would not lock.

So I asked some questions. "Of course you also tried to lock the other front door?" "Yes, yes! That's irrelevant!" She repeated her original question, but with a scorching glance that said I was not measuring up. Now I studied her. It was easy to imagine her as an authoritarian high-school teacher

The woman repeated her original question, but with a scorching glance that said I was not measuring up. Now I studied her.

who considered her students little more than six-year-olds. And me too.

"There does seem to be a connection between the battery and the door locks," I pressed. "That's irrelevant!" And dutifully, she intoned her original question.

Examining her more carefully, I decided I liked her. She was some character! Patiently, I said, "Maybe not. How old is the battery?"

"Oh, I don't know. I'd have to look through all these papers." She indicated a clear, two-gallon plastic bag on her lap, serving as a hand rest for typing. It bulged with papers. They appeared to be jammed in, in no particular order.

"I've left the car lights on before, and the car always started," she added glumly.

"Cold weather is very hard on batteries," I said. "This is our first real cold spell. A four-year-old car battery, for example, would not be reliable in a Minnesota winter. If you recharged the battery or got a new one, the car doors would probably lock again."

Some day she will step from under the cast of her own shadow and find the Light of God. Her life will then be transformed.

With a final shot at being in control of her life, she said, "I grew up in Minnesota, lived my whole life here, but I'm moving!"

"Where to?"

"Not Florida, and not Arizona."

Not, not! Poor wandering Soul, so tied up in knots. She existed in such a cloud of negativity. Some day she will step from under the cast of her own shadow and find the Light of God. Her life will then be transformed.

When I passed her an hour later, she was shouting at someone on her cell phone about her plans to ride city buses home.

This dead-car-battery experience was a marker of her spiritual condition too. A new battery would do her car and her a lot of good. Then she would be able to get up and go again, to a new, higher state of being. If she chose to.

And that would be relevant!

*   *   *

"Ajani" is a Nigerian who, like me, was also out and about. He loves to tell others about Eckankar, so he had put on his ECK T-shirt.

A gentle young man resting on his car door stirred when he read the words "God is love" on Ajani's T-shirt, with an symbol and "Eckankar" printed on the front.

"Are you an ECKist by birth or by choice?" he asked.

Both, explained Ajani. He had been born to ECK parents, but they had left Eckankar due to life's many challenges. Ajani, however, had chosen to stay.

The fellow said he was a Christian, yet he advised Ajani to remain an ECKist.

"I have studied many religions," the young man said. He had come to the conclusion that Eckankar was largely truth. Most people, he believed, go to a religion thinking it will solve all their problems. When the problems remain, they are disappointed. So they leave and go elsewhere.

People, he continued, should go to church for truth. They should not expect their church to provide them with riches and other material things.

This was relevant truth from a very spiritual young man.

He could have taught a lot to the woman men-

A gentle young man resting on his car door stirred when he read "God is love" on Ajani's T-shirt, with an symbol and "Eckankar" printed on the front.

tioned earlier about how to deal with the challenges of living. Or would she dismiss such advice with a snappish, "That is irrelevant!"?

But someday she will break free of her karmic knots.

24
Connections

"Mark" lives in a small Nigerian town once run by crooked politicians, who took people's money meant to improve water supplies, schools, roads, hospital, etc. But those officials had used the money to line their own pockets.

The people were outraged. The townspeople, all Christian, nominated and elected Mark as the new president of the town, because he was an ECKist, known for absolute honesty and for living his religion.

The old guard made repeated attempts to get him to sign away the town's rights and money, to continue the graft. He flatly refused as many times. At year's end, the town's fund held a large surplus. The citizens were delighted. They had made the connection that Mark was a channel for the Inner Master, whom they now call the messiah of the community.

Let us switch gears now.

"Lin" grew up in a family that had the usual ups and downs. Then, her father, at age fifty-two, was diagnosed with bipolar disorder. It is characterized by mood swings, from depression to mania, from being down in the dumps to wild exuberance.

The townspeople, all Christian, made the connection that Mark was a channel for the Inner Master, whom they now call the messiah of the community.

Family life had, of course, been like a roller-coaster ride as her father's disorder had gradually taken hold.

One day, during the worst of an attack, he became psychotic and threatened to kill Lin's mother, and nearly succeeded. This broke up the home. He landed in a psychiatric ward for an extended stay. Her mother was forced to sell the house and move into an apartment.

Even after his release, he had many relapses. Lin's mother suffered greatly in body, mind, and spirit—though she would no longer live with him. She feared for her life.

In time, however, her parents did renew their friendship—probably, Lin feels, because of a very deep love for one another.

Both had since died, some years ago. But Lin was left scarred by the upheaval and violence her father had caused. She could not find it in her heart to forgive him, to ever say, "I love you." Nor did she expect to be able to do so.

However, the Mahanta, the Dream Master, had other plans. He determined that she was now ready to move on to a new spiritual plane.

So he gave her a dream.

Awakening in a beautiful world of light, Lin found herself walking along a road. Off in the distance came a young couple holding hands.

Awakening in a beautiful world of light, Lin found herself walking along a road. Off in the distance came a young couple holding hands, her father and mother in their spiritual bodies. Her father, though, had been healed of his earthly disease and aberrations. His eyes were now clear and calm.

The couple emanated total inner peace, harmony, and love. Her mother had completely forgiven her father, and Lin knew they were again able to live together in their new home.

Telepathically, they asked forgiveness for all the grief they had caused her so long ago.

Lin suddenly felt totally healed. Gone was all the bitterness and resentment that had built up in her heart over the years. And the vibrations were so high, there was no room in her for anything but pure divine love.

For the first time in her life, she was able to say, "Dad, I love you."

Joy filled her when she awoke from this wonderful dream next morning, a dream courtesy of the Mahanta, the Dream Master.

The Master had made a life-changing connection for her with her departed parents.

Joy filled her when she awoke from this wonderful dream. The Master had made a life-changing connection for her with her departed parents.

"Holly" was a soldier in Iraq and there witnessed many horrible things. Just before her deployment, she had lost her younger sister, so she was already in terrible condition even before departure. But a valuable connection was about to be made.

Upon returning to the States, she was ordered to see a therapist, chosen at random in her area. She had post-traumatic stress disorder (PTSD).

Every time she saw "Patrice," it was as if all the pain and hurt in her body had melted away. There was such peace in her office. Holly has seen auras her whole life, but Patrice's was the most beautiful she had ever seen. A brilliant white.

A lady who knew Patrice once said hateful things about her, because she was an ECKist. She further asserted that Eckankar was exclusionary. Not everyone was welcome. Holly knew that was not Patrice at all. At the next treatment session, Holly asked tons of questions about ECK. Satisfied with the answers, she became an ECKist also. The two remain the best of friends.

PTSD still flared up, and Holly also suffered a serious motorcycle crash, but it let her catch a glimpse of a large picture of a place so bright and happy.

That vision finally convinced Holly to live that life right here, right now.

Connections. Just the right connections.

Connections.
Just the right
connections.

Lucy said to the kids, "The Holy Spirit has given us an unexpected gift today that we can take with us for the rest of our lives."

CHAPTER SIX

Every Moment to Its Fullest

25
Young or Old,
It Does Not Matter

I love stories about people who do old things in new ways. Here are two of those stories.

The first is from Dayton Hyde's *The Pastures of Beyond*, an excellent memoir about an Old West that no longer exists. At the time of writing, Hyde was already an old cowhand. One incident he recalled, however, ranged back to him as a sixteen-year-old, six-foot-five beanpole, with already three years of solid cowboying to his credit. He was no greenhorn.

One day, the ranch foreman partnered him with an old cowboy well into his seventies. Hyde pitied Roy as he mounted from a stump, then groaned as he settled his creaking bones into a well-worn saddle.

They were to help out at Klamath Marsh, in southwestern Oregon.

Miles from nowhere when Roy's horse took lame, Hyde resigned himself to a night camping out in a nearby pine forest.

But Roy had other ideas.

He had observed a herd of wild horses moving

Sixteen-year-old Hyde pitied Roy as he mounted from a stump, then groaned as he settled his creaking bones into a well-worn saddle.

115

below them, headed toward a peninsula to drink. "Maybe I'll just get me another horse," said Roy.

Hyde thought the old man was crazy. Catching and breaking a wild horse before sundown?

When the herd saw the two riders emerge from the forest behind them, they stampeded out onto the spur. The old lead mare saw the trap too late. In a panic, she plunged into the swamp, but frightened by the uncertain footing, she scrambled back to shore, then charged the cowboys.

Their loops were not ready. The kid's caught a willow branch. But the old man's riata snagged a big, battle-scarred gray stallion, desperate to join its harem fleeing into the forest. Hyde's ground loop now caught its hind legs and downed it.

A wild fight had ensued. During it, the five-foot, four-inch Roy had transferred his saddle, bit, and bridle to the angry, thrashing stud.

"You think I'm going to ride that horse," the kid snapped, "you're crazy as hell!"

"*You* ride him?" Roy laughed. "I'm going to show you a thing or two. Being young or old doesn't matter half as much as knowin' how."

Roy barked out final orders. Hyde was to free the stud's hind legs when Roy was ready to spring into the saddle, then be sure to keep the wild horse in the marsh water. All was ready.

Once free and in the water, the horse bucked and screamed in rage. It lost its footing, and both man and steed vanished under the boiling water, then popped up, only to disappear again. This happened several more times. The stud even pinned Roy under water at one point, but he pulled the animal's nose under too. It quickly regained its feet.

Roy laughed. "I'm going to show you a thing or two. Being young or old doesn't matter half as much as knowin' how."

Meanwhile, Hyde kept the horse from shore.

After a quarter of a mile following the shoreline, Roy sensed that the animal was ready.

"Ride right in front of him," he said. "Lead him ashore. I think he'll follow your horse." And it did: caught and broken before sundown. The old cowboy had him a mighty fine mount, all because he had recognized and taken advantage of all the tools that the Spirit of life had placed within his reach.

Roy had marshaled all his creative, divine powers. Living every moment to its fullest, he was hardly ready for a retirement home.

Our second example of meeting a problem with a fresh approach is from The Great Courses (thegreatcourses.com) lecture series "Effective Communication Skills," by Professor Dalton Kehoe of York University in Toronto, Ontario. His field is social psychology.

He is a senior partner in a consulting firm that helps organizations reengage their employees.

On one occasion, a company wanted him to help make its managers' meetings more lively and productive. Kehoe sensed that walls of fear and uncertainty separated the people from one another. How could he melt those walls?

He set out to establish what he calls an "appreciative mind-set" in the room. The idea was for each person "to see the useful, desirable, or positive aspects that already exist in the current situation . . . and to know that these can be revealed, evoked, or realized if we ask the right question."

That was the challenge.

Kehoe asked each unit manager to recount one thing that had gone really right since the last meeting.

Roy had marshaled all his creative, divine powers. Living every moment to its fullest, he was hardly ready for a retirement home.

The first few responses were muted and cautious.

But as some amazing and even funny stories were told, the managers began to laugh and really put a lot of enthusiasm and spirit into the session.

The room lit up with productive ideas. Moreover, the people looked forward to similar meetings in the future.

ECKists learn to shortcut the years it might otherwise take. That key is HU.

In these stories, both Roy and Dalton Kehoe had tapped into the creative force that supplies all life. These two were rare in that. Except for ECKists, of course. They learn to shortcut the years it might otherwise take to acquire the experience needed to meet every challenge.

That key is HU.

It is an ancient name for God. Anyone may sing it when there is trouble, stress, or worry. It is sung aloud or silently as HU ("hue"), or also spelled out, H-U. Spiritual aid will come.

Young or old can sing it. Age does not matter.

26
This Is the Gift!

"*Lucy*" benefited from the Mahanta's gift even before she became an ECKist. Later, she could see his hand in guiding her to act in a way that turned a looming disaster into a joyous occasion.

Lucy's daughter had used illegal drugs. The girl was thirteen, and her explorations had landed her in a drug rehabilitation program, where she spent most of her day and had her schooling. It was now just before Thanksgiving Day. Lucy was a volunteer with the rehab program, and the staff knew her. So they agreed to let six of the rehab youth come to Lucy's home for Thanksgiving dinner.

Then, a cloud on the horizon. Her boyfriend at the time, "Ron," dropped in while Lucy and her three kids were preparing dinner. He had brought a folding table at which to seat everyone.

A word about Ron: He was usually a good-hearted person. But a veteran of Vietnam, he had physical and mental scars, which sometimes caused him to fly into a rage at the least provocation. Some little annoyance lit his fuse that day.

Very angry, he shouted at the top of his lungs and pulled the tablecloth from the table, hurling

Lucy could see the Mahanta's hand in guiding her to act in a way that turned a looming disaster into a joyous occasion.

119

the silverware onto the floor. Ron then folded up his table and stormed out the door, slamming it shut behind him.

Silence. Total, shocked silence.

Oh, great! thought Lucy. *What now?*

A nudge came that she later realized had come to her from the Mahanta, the Inner Master. Why not, he said, turn this potential disaster into a special event?

With a smile, she broke the silence.

"OK, now on to Plan B," she said. "Kids, we are going to have some fun!" She ran to the linen closet, placed a large bedsheet on the floor, put the tablecloth on it, then made an announcement. "This is our new table."

So they brought all the food down on the table-cloth and sat cross-legged to eat.

Then Lucy said to them, "We have this oppor-tunity to not only enjoy our dinner, to be grateful for each other's company, and to be grateful for the blessings in our lives, but the Holy Spirit has given us an unexpected gift today that we can take with us for the rest of our lives. And because this gift was given to us in such a dramatic way, I expect none of us will forget it."

The Inner Master, who is spiritually akin to the Holy Spirit, prompted Lucy to say a few more words to her six visitors. Most were from troubled homes.

"This is the gift," she continued. "If someone ever tries to take the table from under you, always have another place to put the tablecloth and go on with your life. Don't allow someone else's bit-terness or anger to take the peace and the love from your heart.

"OK, now on to Plan B," Lucy said. "Kids, we are going to have some fun!"

"In life, we don't have much control over what other people will say, do, or how they will behave, but we do have control on how we understand it and let it affect us."

That immediately changed the mood in the room. The youth began to tell how in the past they had let other people's attitudes affect how they felt about themselves.

Lucy noticed a healing taking place. It was a feeling of being on holy ground, a feeling she would notice many times over in the future as a member of Eckankar. It occurs when someone invites the ECK, the Holy Spirit, into a situation to handle it. The atmosphere inside and outside one changes.

Lucy noticed a healing taking place. It was a feeling of being on holy ground.

So much had the mood lifted, in fact, that the group raised their apple-juice glasses in a toast to Ron.

"We hope you can let your anger cool and also enjoy your Thanksgiving!" This toast and spirit of forgiveness was quite a marvelous step for these youth, whose parents may have been on drugs, were fighting each other, or just were not around.

The evening had turned out much better than Lucy could ever have imagined.

Yet there was a lingering concern. What would happen when the youth shared their Thanksgiving-dinner experience with the rehabilitation staff? Would they ever trust her again to provide a safe environment for the kids?

But Lucy had worried for nothing.

The youth, it turned out, were more impressed with how they had shifted gears than with the actual disruption.

And when it came right down to it, one of the

rehab counselors thought that Lucy had probably staged the disruption to give the young people this experience. But that was hardly the case.

She had asked and the Mahanta had answered.

Lucy observed that after she joined Eckankar, the answers often came readily whenever she asked.

That Thanksgiving Day, she now realized, she had asked and the Mahanta had answered. It was as simple as that.

And that was the gift!

27
Problems and Their Resolutions

*A*lexander Graham Bell, the American inventor who came up with the telephone, said that when one door closes, others open. But he also wisely observed that people's focus is so intent upon the closed doors that they often fail to see the open ones.

Such is true as a general rule. However, there are exceptions. The fact is that individuals have developed many different levels of discrimination over the ages.

Jean de La Fontaine, the French poet known for his fables, tells of an ancient philosopher who once made plans to travel abroad. He wanted to broaden the horizons of his knowledge. So he left his austere home in Scythia, north and northeast of the Black Sea. Soon he arrived in Greece.

In an orchard he saw its owner, a happy and contented man. The philosopher was enamored by the pastoral scene.

The peasant was hard at work with a billhook, a pruning tool. He was lopping branches from a fruit tree, thinning them to let in the sunshine.

People's focus is so intent upon the closed doors that they often fail to see the open ones.

123

The philosopher said, "Why this massacre? It makes no sense to cripple this healthy tree. Let nature take its course. All too soon, this tree will die like everything else. It turns to kindling wood in due season. So put aside your instrument of destruction!"

The philosopher was pleased with his prudent advice about living in harmony with nature.

Even so, the peasant looked at him in wonder, then said in turn, "I only prune what isn't needed. It may look odd to an untrained eye, but the branches I remove allow the tree to bear more bounty. This pruning makes the tree stand stronger!"

When the philosopher returned to his dreary homeland, he told his friends and neighbors of what he had learned in Greece about pruning. He then grabbed a billhook and began to thin his fruit trees. He lopped off branches, needed or not. To make sure he had done a thorough job, he went over his trees once more, to the great consternation of his audience.

The resolution to a problem also depends upon an individual's attitude. Is it upbeat or downbeat?

Shocked by his wild abandon, they advised more prudence in his pruning. But confident of his new knowledge, he shut his ears to their warnings and thus destroyed his entire orchard.

La Fontaine's story of the philosopher is an overdrawn example of discrimination run amok.

In any case, good judgment does differ. People will try to resolve problems in a manner that seems best to them. As ads for products will sometimes caution: "Results may vary!" They may, indeed.

Closed doors, open doors.

The resolution to a problem also depends upon an individual's attitude. Is it upbeat or downbeat?

Recently, I went to my dentist for the replacement of a crown. He did the prep work. Charity, his assistant, would put in the temporary crown. She is a skilled technician, with one of the most upbeat attitudes you could ever imagine.

For example, glue for fastening a temporary crown gets in places on the crown's surface that could irritate a patient. So Charity tries to remove the glue.

In my case, the glue was acting in accordance with its adhesive properties. This did not deter Charity. She scraped and polished the temporary crown, struggling mightily to resolve the problem of glue in the wrong places. "It likes you," she said simply. It took me a moment to catch the real meaning: "I'm having a time of it trying to get this glue off places it shouldn't be."

Charity was forever upbeat. When I was to do my part in a procedure, she would be quick to say, "Oh, very good!"

How could one not keep from trying to please a person like that? Joan, my wife, is one of these optimists too. They see possibilities where others see failure. If you think about it, a situation or a condition is what it is. The dawn of a morning is also just what it is. One individual will look to the rising sun in the east with joy and pleasure, while his counterpart looks with foreboding at gathering storm clouds to the west.

It stands to reason, then, that we can be our own best friend or our own worst enemy. A satisfactory resolution to our fears and problems lies in our attitude.

That is what the Spiritual Exercises of ECK are all about. But to be successful, they must be

To be successful, the Spiritual Exercises of ECK must be done with hopeful expectation.

done with hopeful expectation.

To sum up, good discrimination is at the heart of resolving a problem, which, in the end, is little more than you meeting yourself. It takes experiences of the right kind to reach a true spiritual outlook.

Please remember, that is why the Mahanta, the Living ECK Master has come: to help you achieve it.

28
Growing Pains

*L*ife is uncertain; pain is certain.
     We learn best, I think, when we hurt.
We resolve to sidestep more hurting, even if in
doing so we happen to cause an insult to our own
toes. And hurt.

More often, however, we get hurt because we
don't know something: an experience is new; we've
been pushed too far into the unknown. God has
abandoned us. There is no relief. Just grief.

Are we so powerless?

When I was about twenty, our pastor took a
two-week vacation. It usually meant paying another pastor to cover for him. Why not, suggested
an elder, let Jerome and Harold do it? They're
studying for the ministry.

I froze when Dad told me the news. No one
knew of my secret plans to last out two more years
of study, then quit.

A good summer spoiled!

My Sunday came. The church was packed, like
the previous week, the day my cousin Jerome had
conducted his service. We had cousins, and cousins, and cousins—and dads and moms, and grand-
parents.

*Why not,
suggested an
elder, let
Jerome and
Harold cover
for our pastor?
I froze when
Dad told me
the news.*

Our little country church was pleased.

Like a mechanical monkey, I tried to mimic the best of the many pastors I'd observed in Milwaukee, the location of my school. I was to read a short sermon from a book for laymen to read during a pastor's absence.

Mercifully, the service came to an end. I stood at the back entrance to shake hands with well-wishers. Too much tension. Not my bag.

But the disquiet of being pushed to my limits had one more surprise tucked away. An old, rusted car with a ragged cargo of people drew to a stop along the road fronting the church. The driver alighted.

"Where's the pastor?"

The fellow's knowing smile took in my youth, my black-rimmed glasses, my stiffness. God was good to him.

Someone fingered me. The fellow's knowing smile took in my youth, my black-rimmed glasses, my stiffness. God was good to him.

His mouth spewed hardships: no food for his family since yesterday morning; no place to sleep; the car's gas gauge showed low; he could find no work. Would I take up a collection?

My heart had gone out to him. At a loss, I approached a knot of men where Dad was. The men listened as I related the driver's tale.

Then Ernest S., an old farmer, spoke up. "We pay taxes to help people like this. Tell him there's all the help he needs at the county seat. We'll even call the sheriff to send a deputy to show the way."

The men and Dad nodded in full agreement. Thank God, the monkey was off my back.

The driver misread the letup of tension on my face. He beamed. I beamed. We had a solution for his problems. Wait till he heard it.

His reaction startled me.

At mention of "sheriff," his face took on a scowl. Strain laid wrinkles on his forehead. He backed off a step, then turned briskly and made off at a near trot for the car. He spoke a few words to his passengers, then hurriedly drove away.

The farmers continued to observe the car. The church, on a hill, commanded an unobstructed view of the countryside for a good mile in the direction of the car's passage. Their concern was for their unguarded homes.

But the car trundled past all the farms in sight.

My epiphany was that these canny farmers could smell panhandlers as readily as pigs in a sty. They regarded me as only a pup. Conducting a church service didn't make me a man. They knew that. They remembered their own youth and didn't expect more from me.

How little I knew. Such a humbling realization.

Life was a mystery that would turn one page at a time. It knew I was a slow learner. A lesson had to come at me with many faces before I caught on.

Then a new page would turn.

Growing pains are a necessary part of spiritual development. Age should bring wisdom. But the curious, inquiring child within us must stay true to its divine nature.

Spiritually healthy people keep their faces ever looking ahead, in spite of all self-doubt.

Spiritually healthy people keep their faces ever looking ahead, in spite of all self-doubt.

29
It's a God Thing

*T*here *is* a spiritual lesson in this story. It showcases the spark of creativity, Soul's divine legacy.

"Lee" bikes. One day it occurred to him to get an electric assist for his bike, to give a little help with uphill biking. Wheels began to spin in his head. He'd make a search. But that showed the kinds of bike he wanted started at $6000 and went up to infinity.

Now what?

After scratching his head awhile, he made a decision. Why, he'd build his own! Travails begun.

The start was indeed promising. A frame turned up that cost a tenth of a European frame. So far, so good. He teamed up with techies at a nearby electric bike shop. He'd make a part in his shop. They'd study it at their shop and, often as not, have a better idea.

Next problem, the motor. Resolved. And so on.

Finally, the bike pros called to report they'd overcome the very last hitch. Come and get it.

A genuine Frankenbike (think, chariot of Frankenstein). It surpassed Lee's wildest dreams. How it could eat up hills! A wonder of innovation, and two years of trial and error ended. Stunned relief.

But wait! A wrench in the works?

After miles of rides, he finally plugged in the charger, but the battery stayed uncharged.

More testing and switching of plugs from this to that—and back again—ensued. So the bike guys checked out the charger. It proved defective. A replacement recharged the battery. Now, a really fine electric bike.

In reviewing those last two years, he wondered, *What was all* that *about?*

One night on the inner planes, one of the ECK Masters gently explained that the charger was much like him. He was to pour divine love out so others could benefit from it. Otherwise, he was as useless as a broken bicycle charger.

Lee said, "How can I pour out a flood of divine love I don't have?"

The ECK Master smiled. "It's a God thing. If you give it, it will be.

"Where does the battery get its power? Not from the charger, only through it. When the battery's charge falls low, it draws just the right amount of power through the charger from the source.

"The charger doesn't store up power; it only delivers the correct amount where it's needed. Be like that."

Lee woke up wanting to be a working charger more than anything. He still does.

So his bike-building experience was a spiritual one. He now wonders, *What then isn't a spiritual experience?*

The next pair of stories asks, "A Vahana can

Lee said, "How can I pour out a flood of divine love I don't have?" The ECK Master smiled. "It's a God thing. If you give it, it will be."

do *what?*" The answer may surprise you.

"Ann" and "Bill" had often linked important occasions in their lives—like their honeymoon—to ECK events or seminars. But her health now allowed for fewer such options. Nevertheless, they were still mobile. Since her lungs craved ocean air, they made plans to stay at an oceanside hotel.

Notably, they invited the Master to use them to let others know of ECK.

At the hotel they met a warmhearted woman, "Liz." Ann and Liz were drawn to each other at once. Liz said she'd come with her seventeen-year-old nephew, Eric, who was going through rough times. Fearful, he had few friends, and among the closest was his aunt, middle-aged, never married, and no children.

Ann explained that the special bond some Souls have with each other usually sprang from past-life associations. But Liz, a devout Christian, wouldn't buy it.

Nonetheless, their mutual love surmounted any differences of theology between them, much like a dog and a cat at the same food dish.

"My husband and I would love to speak with your nephew," Ann offered.

Liz said she'd try to arrange it.

Ann and Bill were on the deck, eyes shut, and inwardly singing *HU*. When they finally opened their eyes, Eric was there on the deck. He said his aunt had told him they wished to speak with him.

He reported that he often went to Bible class with his aunt, but he wasn't sure how to connect with Jesus and receive his support and love.

Here was a chance to guide a truth seeker.

Ann and Liz's mutual love surmounted any differences of theology between them, much like a dog and a cat at the same food dish.

A little over an hour later, they had taught him to sing the HU. They'd also spoken to him about the spiritual principles and how to be closer to his teacher, Jesus, and have experiences with him.

What a joy, Eric!

Next day, Ann and Bill drove to a seafood buffet. But a storm had rolled in during their meal, with near-tornadic winds. Not the weather for driving.

Ann said to Bill, "Yesterday we were vehicles for Jesus. Today, for Buddha. Are we doing something wrong?" Not at all. It's a God thing.

So they observed the vicious storm from the restaurant's lobby. Thunder rocked the place. Rain blown nearly horizontal.

The restaurant manager came over and made them feel at ease. A Buddhist, he shared some of his spiritual experiences which he'd told no one before, because he sensed they'd understand. So they taught him how to sing *HU* too. It'd help him link with his teacher and understand some of his experiences.

Later, Ann said to Bill, "Yesterday we were vehicles for Jesus. Today, for Buddha. Are we doing something wrong?"

Not at all. It's a God thing.

Displaying the words "ECK" and "Eckankar" in our public postings is a gift of love to seekers, to allow them to begin or continue the divine passage home to God.

CHAPTER SEVEN

Love In, Love Out

30
Serving a Snapping Turtle—and Others

To become more spiritual, we must serve others.

To fly higher, we must reach out a helping hand to others.

To get more love, we must give more love to others.

An easy way is to open your heart to the Inner Master's bidding, and divine love will take over, right before your eyes.

"Rose" shares an example with us. She was driving home on her lunch hour, when she decided to be fully conscious of the ECK, the Holy Spirit. No car radio. No cell-phone calls. Just awareness of God's presence.

Ahead of her, a huge turtle was crossing the road. Rose stopped ten feet from it. Immediately, the Inner Master said, "Don't touch that turtle. Watch what happens."

She understood that she was to remain there as an instrument for the Mahanta, the Inner Master.

A white truck pulled up, and two young men

To fly higher, we must reach out a helping hand to others.

climbed out. One seized the turtle's tail, intending to drag it to safety. His companion shouted, "Don't do that! It's a snapping turtle." Sure enough, the big turtle spun around and made a lunge for the offending hand. Chastened, the fellow drew back, choosing to be a bystander.

While all this was going on, another white truck had pulled up. An older man emerged.

He surveyed the situation and went to the back of his truck for an eight-foot ladder. He and the other young man each took an end. Then they used it to corral the turtle, pushing it to the lake's side of the road, its destination.

The turtle disputed the proceedings every foot of the way. Snap, snap, snap.

What did Rose take away from all this?

While the men shepherded the turtle to safety, Rose was inwardly singing *HU* as she directed traffic around them. She thanked the men for their help. They shrugged off her thanks with a very Minnesotan "Oh, sure." Then a wave of love embraced all three.

Rose recognized what a precious gift of service it is to help a Soul on Its journey to God. Even if it happens to be a snapping turtle.

She recognized what a precious gift of service it is to help a Soul on Its journey to God. Even if it happens to be a snapping turtle.

"Janet" is an ECK leader who serves a remote area in Canada. It was evening and also time to call all the seekers on her contact list to invite them to the monthly Sound of Soul event. But Janet was tired. She toyed with the idea of putting it off, since she had come home from a grueling workday. She could let these calls slide a month, couldn't she?

Laying the tempting thought aside, she began dialing Mary, first on the list.

Mary had received some ECK materials but had not yet attended a Sound of Soul event. Mary could hardly believe her ears. "You will never understand how important your call is at this very moment," she said to Janet.

Mary had just pulled off the road. Her car had seemed not in proper order somehow. It is against the law in Canada to use a cell phone while driving. Just then, hers rang.

She was afraid to be on the highway after dark. Worse, snow was beginning to fall.

Her brother had passed on a few days earlier, and she was on her way to tie up loose ends for him. She had barely the money to meet this month's rent. Now this! How could she manage the added expenses of settling his affairs? She began to cry.

Only moments before Janet's call, she'd asked for God's help.

Through her tears she asked Janet to sing *HU* for her, since she was too upset. Several minutes later, however, Mary joined in. By the time Janet ended the call with "May the blessings be," Mary had been transformed. She was now fit to continue the journey.

Janet sat back in awe of the subtle workings of the Inner Master. The timing of her call had been perfect. She vowed to never again hesitate to do the Master's work.

There was a bonus too. The Sound of Soul event in her small city had seven guests and seven ECKists.

She says it is an amazing gift from the Mahanta to serve and help others experience the HU.

"Edgar" hails from Nigeria. Three months earlier, he was transferred to busy and noisy Lagos.

Janet sat back in awe of the subtle workings of the Inner Master. She vowed to never again hesitate to do the Master's work.

He works with three Christian women in his new office. They were courteous, for the most part.

However, when it came to understanding what Eckankar is about, they would all "scamper."

One day, he decided to do a favor for one named Rose. So he installed a Bible-verse program on her computer that randomly displays quotes from the Bible. Five minutes later, a strong fragrance wafted into every corner of the office. It was the scent of camwood, also known as African sandalwood.

When Edgar feels sad, it comforts him. It is his special communication link to ECK Master Rebazar Tarzs. Usually, he alone can detect it. This time, though, Rose could too. She sniffed everywhere.

Our service to God will call up some unusual situations.

He said she must be lucky to have this gift from God. She, on the other hand, thinks he performed some kind of magic. In time, she'll understand.

Our service to God will call up some unusual situations. Here, serving a snapping turtle—and others.

31
Serving You!

pharmacy runs an ad on a local radio station that lacks two words to be a more effective closing line.

The store touts the high quality of its customer service. And well it should. When a parent with a sick child drops in with the child in tow, the parent finds the prescription right at the front of the store. There is no need to march past rows of enticing merchandise on a long walk to the back of the place. So it is a quick in and a quick out.

The pharmacy will even deliver prescriptions right to a home. It truly is a service-driven organization.

Unfortunately, to my mind, the announcer's punch line forgets the customer, who should be part of it. So the ad closes weakly, like this: "Doing what *we* do best." How would it sound with "serving you" tacked on?

"Doing what we do best, serving *you!*"

Now my tummy feels better. No more waiting for the other shoe to drop.

It is exactly the same attitude an ECKist adopts when serving the ECK or humanity.

Serving God and life is, at its heart, a selfless

"Doing what we do best, serving you!" is exactly the attitude an ECKist adopts when serving the ECK or humanity.

143

commitment. *The Shariyat-Ki-Sugmad*, Book One, says: "Many have been called but few are able to comprehend and understand the ECK. Those Souls who do are then consciousnesses that are open to the ECK for gaining awareness. They serve in the lower worlds, or wherever Soul is needed."

All right, your day is a mad gallop from the moment you roll out of bed in the morning until you find it again come night. Where is there time to serve? Run, run, run, run.

Service starts at home.

At the very least, make some day special for you, a family member, or the whole family. Celebrate a special day, like a birthday, an anniversary, or a just-because day. Make plans. Do something new or some favorite seldom-time-for activity like going to a movie, an ice-cream shop, or maybe for a walk in the park.

If such things can reawaken you to the sheer joy of being alive—wonderfully, vibrantly, gratefully alive—then they are spiritual.

Hey, wait a minute! How are these things spiritual service?

If such things can reawaken you to the sheer joy of being alive—wonderfully, vibrantly, gratefully alive—then they are spiritual. Plan for more like moments and days.

That addresses service to you, family, and friends.

Two other areas of service include what we do for God and what we do for others, apart from family and friends.

The highest service is serving the Sugmad. Those able to do this are the ECK Masters. When Soul enters the region of Light that is the Kingdom of the Sugmad, "It either remains or is given a mission somewhere in the lower kingdom," says *The Shariyat-Ki-Sugmad*, Book One. "But It knows immortality and the joy of serving with the Sugmad to keep the vast universes running smoothly."

And such is your goal.

The ECK Masters enjoy a wide range of freedom, able to come and go in the Soul body as they please. They assure the uncertain to follow through with some plan to enter a new level of spiritual awareness.

Very often an ECK Master will simply accompany a chela on an adventure in the Far Country. It is enjoyable for student and Master alike.

The God Worlds are, well, fun! Just be aware, I am always there with you.

The God Worlds are, well, fun! Just be aware, I am always there with you.

Finally, there is the wide-open area of service to others. The sky is the limit. Look around. Do you see any opportunities? Service to other people begins with you and your situation. Have wealth but little time? Write a check to an organization noted for making good, not wasteful, aid available to the needy.

"Andy," a ninety-one-year-old, is a resident in a retirement home. He serves the Mahanta there, nobly and well. But he has a problem. Let us see what it is.

For a long time, he felt a yearning to leave the home, uproot, and move someplace he could enjoy the company of ECKists. But the ECK placed him where he was most needed.

How does he serve?

Andy's broad life experiences make him a good, understanding listener. He does deliver flowers to some hospice patients and sometimes sits with a patient. He visits friends in the hospital. But so do others. Yet staff members tell him he is making a real difference.

Love and be loved as you serve.

So what is the problem?

He is the only ECKist among all his Christian friends and acquaintances. A gnawing fear: will he let the Mahanta down?

Not a chance, Andy! Love and be loved as you serve.

32

Resist God's Will?

*L*ove will have us when we give up and let go. "Kelly" is an acupuncturist in a remote, very conservative, Christian town. Being an ECKist, she wisely keeps her head down. She has found that when she has a cold or some other ailment, when her physical senses are a little blocked, then she is a much clearer channel for the Holy Spirit to flow through.

Maybe it is because there is then less strength to resist God's will. Let's see.

Kelly was in the final stages of clearing out a nagging, fuzzy end-of-cold head. Over the next three days, she would find an opportunity to give three people a HU CD. That is, *HU: A Love Song to God*.

Her ten-o'clock patient that day was a sixty-two-year-old woman. She had come for treatment off and on for three years.

"Do you know of a meditation class I can join?" It was practically the first thing out of her mouth. Kelly's inner voice, the Inner Master, said, "Finally, she's ready!" Kelly was delighted, of course.

So she gave her patient a short intro to ECK, a HU CD, and an invitation to an ECK class beginning in a few weeks.

What a wonderful start to the day!

The very next patient was a surprise too. She was fifty-one. A new patient, she had been in the week before for a tinnitus treatment. Now she said that her tinnitus had changed to the sound of crickets and a variety of different tones.

Kelly just listened. She had not had time to come to know her as either a patient or a person. What dare she say? She kept checking inwardly.

She determined to let the ECK, the Holy Spirit, make the call.

Gently, Kelly asked, "Could it be the Sound of God you are hearing?"

The woman began to cry.

Gently, Kelly asked, "Could it be the Sound of God you are hearing?" The woman began to cry.

"Yes," she said. Kelly asked, "Are you ready to take the next step spiritually?" A still more definite yes. She was tired of holding herself back. Strongly spiritual she knew she was, but she had kept herself from pursuing the spiritual life for much too long.

The two enjoyed a good chat about the different sounds and planes of God. The sound of a cricket is but one of many, many ways that the ECK, the Voice of God, may choose to communicate with Souls like us.

Kelly also gave her a HU CD and an invitation to the ECK class slated for the following month.

A few days later, a patient asked about health as a state of consciousness. Could she change this state? This patient was thirty-four and had been working with sound and color for self-healing. What a perfect opening to introduce the Light and Sound of God to her.

So this person, too, received a HU CD, a brief ECK intro, and an invitation to the upcoming class.

What was Kelly's take-away from all this?

It correctly appears to her that the more we give of ourselves to others, the more we find answers to our own questions about life.

Resist God's will? No. Just be a true public servant and serve others spiritually.

Just be a true public servant and serve others spiritually.

33
Love In, Love Out

*W*e go forward in life confident and assured that all is as it should be. Because it is! God loves us.

In return, we serve others. Love in, love out. God's love comes in, so we find outlets for it. Illustrations follow:

God's love comes in, so we find outlets for it.

Our first story is from a chela who never suspected that an old, stubborn attitude was restricting the ECK Current going through her: self-will.

"Jean" is a practical nurse. Her area of service is elderly care in the home.

She counted on going to a major ECK seminar, which meant working ahead. So she was constantly on the run. Jean was operating with the premise that if she did all in Sugmad's name, events would just glide along. It was a sort of "deal." All would then flow smoothly, seamlessly. Self-will had it all worked out.

Instead, the intensity dial was turned up the weekend before the ECK seminar. Everything fell apart around her.

The weekend saw two patients at home from the emergency room (ER) that required her close attention. But unanticipated was yet another admission to the ER on Monday, and a second on Tuesday. In addition, a third patient needed urgent care at home. And so it went.

In the end, Jean made her flight. She was also able to attend all the seminar events she'd planned on.

She later realized that when she'd opened herself as a channel for divine love, the ECK gave her more opportunities to bring the Light and Sound of God to her patients and their families. The ECK had blessed her with a calm, peaceful heart and a sense of humor to get her through those trying preseminar days.

Freed also of her self-will and "deal making" with the ECK, she felt lighter and more free to move on to greater spiritual opportunities.

Love in, love out.

A reminder now about the great importance of the words "ECK" and "Eckankar." Displaying them in our public postings is a gift of love to seekers, to allow them to begin or continue the divine passage home to God.

In times past, "Lois" has been distressed to see postings for Eckankar events that omitted the words "ECK" and "Eckankar." The words are dynamic. They are always to be visible.

Lois offers firsthand experience in that regard.

She was browsing in a bookstore when a voice behind her stammered, "Whh . . . what does that word on your hoodie mean?" The voice's owner was a girl of about thirteen or fourteen. She stood frozen in her tracks.

"What word, my dear?"

"On your hoodie . . . 'Eckankar.' What does it mean? I don't understand. I feel so confused all of

Freed of her self-will and "deal making" with the ECK, Jean felt lighter and more free to move on to greater spiritual opportunities.

a sudden. Is it a church, a school, or someone's name? What is it? I don't know why I feel so confused."

Checking inwardly with Z, the Inner Master, Lois knew she was not to interfere with this youth's choice of faith, or the girl's upbringing by the parents.

"It's the name of my church," she said gently.

The girl's expression and the light in her eyes were a blend of wonder, love, confusion, grace, and peace. It was clear she'd made the inner connection with the ECK. Then she scampered off to rejoin her mother.

This experience recalled for Lois her own, initial encounter with the words "ECK" and "Eckankar" when near this girl's age.

She was at a huge flea market. Frequently, she dashed ahead of the neighbor's family she'd come with, to look at the mixture of antiques, jewelry, rusty tools, furniture, and just plain junk that people were trying to sell.

Suddenly, she stood fixed to the spot. "Eckankar" was the only word on a huge banner over a booth. What was that word?

Confused and amazed, she numbly accepted the booklets and brochures a man held out for her. Right then, the family she was with had caught up.

"Whatcha got there?"

Embarrassed and afraid of others' opinions, she stuffed the smallest brochure in her pocket, dropping the rest into a trash can. Never again did she see the Eckankar booth at the flea market. And only years later did she find the ECK teachings again.

The girl's expression and the light in her eyes were a blend of wonder, love, confusion, grace, and peace.

Let people hear and see "ECK" and "Eckankar." Their immediate response or reaction is of no concern to you, because their spiritual unfoldment alone determines when they will embrace the ECK teachings.

Love in, love out.

34
Learning about ECK

*H*elping people find a new means of reaching out for divine love and truth is a real pleasure.

Did "Candi" encounter an ECK Master while still a teen?

She once attended a concert with a somewhat irresponsible date, who forgot where he'd parked the car.

Midnight saw the concert ended and the forlorn couple wandering up one parking lot aisle and then down another. Hopeless. It was a high-crime area, and Candi was understandably fearing for their safety.

A figure suddenly materialized from the gloom. "Do you need help finding your car?"

Cheerful, and carrying a good feeling about him, he proceeded to walk ahead of them, hands clasped behind his back. His suit and tie had further secured the trust of Candi and her friend.

Finally, the stranger asked, "Is this your car?"

It was. They were overjoyed to have it located and get home. Then she forgot the entire incident.

Years later, she found Eckankar. A photo of Paul Twitchell, the modern-day founder of Eckankar,

A figure suddenly materialized from the gloom. Cheerful, and carrying a good feeling about him, he proceeded to walk ahead of them.

recalled the memory of that fearful night of searching for a lost car.

The photo reminded her of their benefactor, as did Paul's recorded voice.

She thought, *Wow! Could that have been the ECK Master Paul Twitchell?* It seemed likely, but she remained undecided.

Paul might have told her to determine the answer herself, because such was often his response to others with similar misgivings.

The ECK Masters urge people to take responsibility for their own decisions.

The ECK Masters urge people to take responsibility for their own decisions.

"Renée" has a singular story of how she learned about the teachings of ECK. It begins sad but ends well.

Her life's journey had conveyed to her many crushing blows, all of which were intended to inspire spiritual growth. When Renée was yet a minor, her divorced mother and her boyfriend devised a scheme to have Renée go online to trap rich older men, to weasel money from their coffers. She was to be the bait.

This dear Soul suffered much physical and emotional grief aiding the two.

But then the hand of ECK revealed Itself in her meeting a kind man online, who said he Soul Traveled. The term meant nothing to her. Over time, they drifted apart.

Finally, she was able to break free of her scheming mother and accomplice.

She obeyed a nudge to again contact her old online friend. It'd been several years. One thing led to another until she found Eckankar. Recently, Renée was also able to forgive her mother, finally understanding that the adversaries in her life were sacred too.

Now on to "Frank."

Frank was en route to an ECK Worldwide Seminar. On the flight, he was to learn more about the subtleties of ECK.

He was seated between two women. The older, well-dressed and stylish, woman, remarked, "Isn't it interesting that you're sitting next to two born-again Christians?" He agreed. He sensed that the Inner Master had plans for this trip.

She had a fear of flying and ordered an alcoholic beverage, after professing to have a strong faith. "But if the plane goes down," she joked, "I'm going to work on you." She meant, try to convert him.

Twice, she tried; twice, he rebuffed her.

On her third attempt, the Inner Master prompted Frank to profess his faith in ECK. He was to take a stand. Words flowed from him.

Life is good. But it's especially good when we can help people discover a new means of reaching out for divine love and truth, the ECK way.

Thoughtfully, she replied, "I see you are a loving person, and you have a strong relationship with God through your faith." Pausing, she added, "I respect your powerful relation to your faith."

She had also learned of ECK.

Frank had taken something from their exchange, too, about the subtleties of the ECK. He learned the necessity of sticking up for one's faith in loving ways that do not invalidate the beliefs of others.

Life is good. But it's especially good when we can help people discover a new means of reaching out for divine love and truth, the ECK way.

All four were humbled by the confluence of events that had graced this day; and for three, learning of HU and Eckankar.

CHAPTER EIGHT

Faith, Love, and Trust

35

Yes, We Can
Reach All Seekers!

"Marta" was the new Vahana coordinator in her area.

She was especially anxious about submitting her first calendar listing to an online magazine.

It took her hours to decipher the vague instructions, then she had to leave messages for the publication before its deadline. After much back and forth, she finally managed to place the ads.

Then, a snag! The online version was OK, but the print copy had a major flaw.

Why was placing the ads such a trial? Was there a reason?

To correct the error for the next two issues at no cost, she planned to go to the publisher's office in person to place the new listings. Before leaving home, she'd felt a nudge to take along three specific Vahana handouts.

The meeting with the publisher ran two and a half hours. The woman had many questions about Eckankar. A local ECK group had once placed ads in this publication, but the publisher had come away with a mistaken notion about ECK.

Why was placing the ads such a trial? Was there a reason?

Marta informed her, "If you're happy with your spiritual path, then that's where you need to be."

Surprisingly, the publisher replied, "I'm not happy with it."

Surprisingly, the publisher replied, "I'm not happy with my spiritual path." So she was a seeker! Her questions tumbled out.

So she was a seeker! As her questions tumbled out, Marta handed her the three ECK handouts, one by one. The woman is now singing the HU with her husband at night and is eager to learn more about ECK.

Now Marta understood the difficulty in placing the online and print ads. The woman needed more time to absorb the reasons Marta loved the ECK so much.

Moving on . . .

"Lise" is a Swiss who traveled to Vienna, Austria, to attend several concerts in the Golden Hall, a renowned venue for classical music. The music in that atmosphere soon moved her to tears. It was divine food. It helped her reconnect with the might of God's love.

On the train ride home, a man sitting next to her shared a flyer of a book he'd written about Gnosticism. A discussion followed. An inner prompting urged her to relate an out-of-body experience she'd once had. Her companion, surprised and interested in her story, wanted to hear all about it.

Before the train reached his stop, he asked for her email address. They are now corresponding; his questions keep flooding in. He's definitely a seeker.

After he left the train, a woman from a nearby compartment, who'd overheard their conversation, asked to share Lise's compartment. For two hours she aired her troubles. Yet she also posed a string of heartfelt questions with a spiritual bent.

Lise presented her with a HU card. The woman wished to exchange phone numbers, since they lived a scant fifty miles apart. She wanted to meet again. If she does call, Lise is ready to follow up, to help another "hound of heaven" in every possible way.

Now let's see what "Jeffrey" was up to.

He and his wife were vacationing on Maui, Hawaii, enjoying their last cup of coffee and muffin outside a coffee shop. An elderly woman approached their table, smiled, and politely greeted them.

Just one look at her bad teeth and disheveled clothes, and the likelihood that she'd ask for money, might have prompted them to tell her to move along. The couple instead returned her greeting and began to chat with her. After some time she revealed that she thought she had a guardian angel. This was Jeffrey's opportunity to ask, "Have you explored the spiritual paths on the island?"

She shook her head.

But when he mentioned Eckankar, her face lit up. She'd discovered it while living in California, but she'd given it up because she couldn't understand *The Shariyat-Ki-Sugmad*, the ECK bible. It was too intellectual for her, a simple person.

Jeffrey quickly enlightened her. He hadn't been able to understand it either at first, but it didn't matter. The vibration of the words alone had opened his heart. That was what Eckankar was about— opening hearts!

That was what Eckankar was about— opening hearts!

No one had ever told her so.

Then she told of an experience with the Light

and Sound. Jeffrey pointed out that the two were why she'd felt a guardian angel was looking after her. She'd been blessed by the ECK, the Light and Sound of God. It had always been with her in this lifetime, although she'd not always pursued a closer bond with It. As a favor, he loaded the HU song on her smartphone and also passed along the time and place of an upcoming Day of ECK.

So what had Jeffrey learned from this meeting?

He now listens to all who come to him, since the Mahanta has likely sent them. He also waits for an opportunity to bring up Eckankar. Mainly, he listens. Finally, he sees that they know how to take another step in ECK should they want to.

During your spiritual exercises, affirm your willingness to be a hand of God, that day and every day.

What is your best way to be a Vahana? During your spiritual exercises, affirm your willingness to be a hand of God, that day and every day.

Many thanks to our three Vahanas for their outstanding stories.

Yes, we can reach all seekers!

36

Faith, Love, and Trust

$\mathcal{I}$t is a pleasure to hear from ECKists who "get it," in regard to love and trust in the Mahanta, the inner side of the Living ECK Master. His intervention often appears during turning points in their lives.

"Emily" is one of those happy Souls. She was laid off during the early cycle of job losses in 2009.

A week prior to her layoff, she recorded a predictive dream that she interpreted as a forewarning of the imminent loss of her job.

Then, on the eve of her layoff, she noted a second dream. This one, another predictive dream, revealed she would land a new job with good pay. Emily points out that for the past month she had asked the Mahanta for a raise in pay.

The next morning she was duly laid off.

Then the fun began.

She tried to be unhappy, but, inexplicably, her exuberance kept bubbling to the surface, wreathing her face in a happy smile. Coworkers thought the shock had flipped her headlong into the stages of denial, acceptance, and all the rest. But when her overwhelming joy continued to show even more, they wrote her off as out of her head.

Emily tried to be unhappy, but, inexplicably, her exuberance kept bubbling to the surface.

165

Emily confided to two colleagues about the HU. She said, "It can give peace of mind and perspective."

One of them embraced the idea, but the other balked. "I'll wait for things to get worse in my life," he scoffed, "before I'll sing the HU!" (To each his own.)

About a week later, she called her old workplace to discuss an apparent error in her final severance pay. The amount seemed low. A human-resources representative said, "There's no discrepancy. You'll see the full explanation in your offer letter." Offer letter? The rep mentioned the offer letter up to four times before correcting herself with, "Sorry, I meant to say income statement."

Offer letter? This bank had just laid her off. Then it dawned on Emily that she was scheduled for an interview later in the day.

Mention of an offer letter plus a job interview was a hint she would get a job.

All along, Emily's love for the Mahanta wavered not once. She had trusted her dreams. And she knew if there was to be more money, it would manifest somewhere down the line.

A first and second interview were safely behind her, with a third in the offing, when she received an offer letter for a new, higher position with the same bank. She now works as a portfolio manager for the central region of her state, at a much higher salary.

All along, Emily's love for the Mahanta wavered not once. She had trusted her dreams. And she knew that if there was to be more money, it would manifest somewhere down the line.

Faith, love, and trust—three keystones of ECK. She had them all.

*   *   *

A recent employee and his wife were new arrivals from a tropical country. (We will call the husband "Brett.") The two came upon a lovely townhome, for a reasonable price, with a commanding view of the Temple of ECK. The woman who wanted to sell it to them was not an ECKist. Nor did she know the name "Eckankar."

However, she said it always comforted her at night, after the door was locked and the kids were in bed, to look over at the Temple and know that all was right with the world.

A surprising thing was that some Eckankar employees had suggested the couple buy something a few miles from the ECK Temple. It was to get a break from the continuous ECK flow near the Temple. A break from it? Brett thought otherwise. He felt that one has to be immersed in the ECK flow to become the HU. He certainly was not looking for a respite from it.

Yes, they had meant well.

The purchase of their home ran into a few communication snags. His old foreign bank refused to transfer the couple's funds to their new Minnesota bank. A delay could risk their closing on the property. Should Brett return to that country to facilitate the matter, or trust his lawyer there to handle the affair?

So he asked the Mahanta for a sign. Both his choices were unlikely to appear: a flag of that country (to go); an elk (to stay).

Thirty seconds later, he spotted an elk on a highway billboard. Then another. A definite sign to stay in Minnesota.

Only later did he learn that the two animals were actually caribou, like reindeer. No matter, they had served the purpose. So he remained in Minnesota; his lawyer arranged the transfer of funds.

The woman was not an ECKist. However, she said it comforted her at night to look over at the Temple and know all was right with the world.

Faith, love, and trust have served Emily and Brett well. They do love the Mahanta.

All is, and will be, as it must be. That is the way of it.

37

The Joy Blotters—
Bringers of Doubt
and Fear

"Roberta," a longtime High Initiate in ECK, tells of something weighing upon her heart.

When an ECK chela receives the gift of another initiation, some thoughtless H.I.'s and longtime ECKists give a knowing look and say, "Wow, now the hard stuff begins; hope you are prepared for it . . ." and other fear-instilling words.

At an ECK Worldwide Seminar, a new member asked a roundtable facilitator, an ECK Spiritual Aide (ESA), why some ECKists would tell her to enjoy the thrill of the new ECK experience because later the hard stuff comes in.

So she asked, "Why does the joy not continue?" Fortunately, the ESA could assure her that the joy does indeed continue.

Roberta says that in her experience, most chelas were ready for the next step, joyful and happy when the pink slip arrived in the mail. That is, until the "joy blotters" got to work. She calls them

Roberta says most chelas were ready for the next step, joyful and happy when the pink slip arrived in the mail.

169

the "bringers of doubt and fear," and why they feel a need for such behavior is more than she can understand.

It gets down to the ceaseless tug of war between love and power.

Here it is fitting to note the ECK axiom to use as a criterion in our interactions with others: "Is it true, is it necessary, is it kind?" Otherwise, don't do it.

Roberta feels that if these people cannot celebrate the spiritual blessing of an ECK initiation and share in this Soul's good fortune, they could at least have the good sense to practice the Law of Silence.

When put-upon Souls come to her with their questions, instilled by doubt, she takes time to point out all the spiritual benefits of the ECK initiation. She further points to the importance of trusting the Inner and Outer Master. "See the gift as one of divine love from the Mahanta. It is a great blessing to be cherished."

Roberta is reminded of *The Shariyat-Ki-Sugmad* where it says that an H.I. must protect all who are eligible to enter the heavenly worlds.

Learn to be a sunbeam and not a rain cloud at others' special events. Be a light, not a shadow; more the smile, less the frown.

Moving into the holy land of divine consciousness entails the development of such attributes as diplomacy and grace. Learn to be a sunbeam and not a rain cloud at others' special events. Be a light, not a shadow; more the smile, less the frown.

"Jen," a student of the ECK teachings under the guidance of the Mahanta, the Living ECK Master, says that she is "ever a beginner, ever a student, *ever encouraging fellow spiritual travelers,* even as she is likewise helped along."

She gives thanks for all the pleasures and

pains, laughter and tears, work and rest.

And also for the successes and failures, gains and losses along the endless path of love, divine love. A Third Initiate of ECK after twelve years in Eckankar, Jen lists the benefits to her of this association with ECK. Here are a few:

- Now, wonder most often trumps worry.
- A "helpless victim" has become author of all her own stories—much nicer stories too!
- Answers to questions and solutions to problems appear without prodding and pleading.
- Past regrets and future unknowns dim in the light of present gifts.
- Work is no longer a duty, rather a privilege, while watching the ECK working Its miracles in Its ways and Its timings.
- Instead of good and bad, all situations are seen as opportunities to learn more about giving and receiving love and service.

You might reread these benefits. These six are only the first third of eighteen; the rest offer equally insightful points. The blessings of insights that rise from being in ECK abound all around Jen. To her credit, she sees them.

We just need to stop, look, and listen.

Joan and I were in the waiting room of a clinic. Near us sat a small man with sparkling and mischievous eyes. He gave his age as "nine . . . three." Ninety-three. Joan asked him to repeat it, because he looked fifteen to twenty years younger.

His second wife had died some thirteen years ago, and now he lived alone. Proudly, he said he cooked his own meals: some meat, fresh vegetables, and a raw salad. And yes, a "shot" of some unnamed beverage before bedtime too.

A "helpless victim" has become author of all her own stories—much nicer stories too!

He chose to walk on the sunny side.

He was a happy, charming man who had undoubtedly seen much tribulation during his ninety-three years, but he chose to walk on the sunny side of the street.

There is a lot to reflect upon in this message to you. I will leave you to it.

38
Being Enthusiastic, Positive, and Giving Freedom

$\mathcal{S}$omeone once asked me, "How do we speak about ECK membership to newcomers?"

I said, "If the enthusiasm and love is within you, they will feel it. If your heart is open, people can tell that you are a genuine person, that you walk the talk."

So how does that play out on the home front?

Two people, whom we will call Cathy and Tim, saw it play out in the following manner. Cathy is a longtime ECKist. She and several other ECKists handed out HU cards at a community event in the area. It was a simple Vahana deed.

One man, in particular, was very interested in the HU card, which stirred his curiosity about Eckankar.

This man's name was Tim. After his second visit to the ECK Center for a HU chant, he joined Cathy and a group of ECKists, who went out for dinner. She sat next to him at the end of the table. Tim told her how he had learned of Eckankar.

If enthusiasm and love is within you, newcomers will feel it.

"Do you have any questions?" she asked. "Do you understand the basics of Eckankar?"

In fact, Tim was eager to hear about the basic philosophies and teachings, and they had a delightful exchange for an hour. But what Cathy found most interesting was what had appealed to him about the teachings of ECK and how they were presented through the chelas he met.

Tim liked to chant *HU*. It felt good. Unlike the chanting he did with another spiritual group, he said the HU was more primal, more basic and simple.

He could feel the energy move through him when he sang it.

At the end of their conversation, Tim said what really caught his attention about the power in the teachings of ECK was Cathy's enthusiasm and that of the woman who had originally given him the HU card. He was simply amazed that Cathy spoke so eagerly about Eckankar after being in it eleven years. In his experience, people who had been in a religion for eleven years—or in anything, for that matter—had lost their enthusiasm for it.

Tim was simply amazed that Cathy spoke so eagerly about Eckankar after being in it eleven years.

There was yet another thing that had struck him. This was what he called the positivity and love the ECKists expressed about the teachings of ECK.

Their approach was positive and uplifting.

Tim said he had grown tired of hearing about hell, sins, damnation, and the like. He added that Eckankar was the first religious teaching he had encountered that focused on love and positivity, and never even brought up hell and sinning.

The old ruses of fear and guilt had worn out their welcome, it would seem, in the house of Tim's state of consciousness.

The Mahanta had freed Tim to make his own judgments.

A third point Tim mentioned is instructive here. He greatly appreciated the fact that no one was forcing Eckankar upon him, so he felt respected and did not feel as if some were pushing their teachings down his throat. That, he could not take.

The Mahanta had freed Tim to make his own judgments.

Cathy was excited about this conversation. Tim had given her valuable feedback about what worked and what did not, observations by an astute student of human nature. More to the point, she felt highly honored that the Master had chosen her to be a vehicle for sharing the ways of ECK with Tim. She often told others about ECK, but this "chance" meeting marked the very first time she had gotten feedback on what worked.

Tim had thus brought up three points that opened him to hearing more about the ECK teachings.

First, Cathy's enthusiasm, as well as her ability to speak about Eckankar clearly.

Second, her focus on the positive.

Third, the freedom and space she gave him, not pushing the teachings in his face.

So what worked in this Vahana effort was enthusiasm, positivity, and freedom. You, like Cathy, now have more clarity about what one newcomer really appreciated about a presentation of the ECK teachings. It is certainly worth keeping in mind.

Natural, then, is another question once posed to me. A High Initiate asked, "Is there any way we can help newcomers get more committed in the first year or so?"

The answer was that the first several years

are a shakeout period. Still, better ECK presentations can prequalify new people before they come into Eckankar. Tell them of the spiritual benefits. On the other hand, remain upbeat and avoid going to extremes. For example, do not say, "Here are the benefits, but your life will go to hell as your karma burns off!"

(This answer drew a hearty laugh from the High Initiate.)

So, be enthusiastic, keep the ECK presentation positive, and above all, give an individual the freedom of his own state of consciousness.

Above all, give an individual the freedom of his own state of consciousness.

39

Be Yourself
and Serve Life

"Cecile" attended workshops at an ECK World-wide Seminar and focused upon her mission: Be yourself and serve life.

Drawn to the park across from the site of the seminar, the Minneapolis Convention Center, she came upon a joyful wedding party gathered for photographs, while golden sunlight splashed the autumn leaves overhead. But the perfection of the moment was suddenly broken.

An angry bicyclist was cursing a car parked at the curb in front of the park's entrance. It was blocking the bike lane.

The driver emerged from the car, explaining, "I'm trying to get these ninety-year-old people out of the car." Then he added, "God bless." Cecile guessed the passengers were the proud grand-parents of the bride and groom. The harsh scolding of the bicyclist had opened the door for her to clear the air by offering an act of kindness to comfort the family.

"Here, let me help you," she said.

Gently she assisted an elderly woman from the

Drawn to the park across from the ECK seminar site, Cecile came upon a joyful wedding party gathered for photographs.

car to the safety of the sidewalk. Noticing the traffic had stalled at the nearby intersection's green light, she began to direct traffic around the parked car. The driver thanked her and sped off.

Cecile was elated by her experience. She practically skipped along the sidewalk, stopping to visit with other ECKists.

After a bit, she observed the driver of the car approaching her on foot. He thanked her again for her intervention. Then he asked, "What group are you with?" He'd apparently linked her behavior to the organization at the seminar.

"Eckankar," she said, holding up her seminar badge so he could see and remember the word. At the same time, her other hand produced a HU card. "We practice singing this beautiful word, *HU*," she explained. "It helps us experience God's love directly, and it brings harmony."

He accepted the card. "I'm pastor for this wedding, and I'm very interested in the spiritual practices of other religions. I will look into this." It turned out he was also father of the bride.

The rudeness of the bicyclist had unwittingly given Cecile a chance to inform the pastor about HU, a higher level in his search for God.

Cecile noted how the rudeness of the bicyclist had unwittingly given her a chance to inform the pastor about HU, a higher level in his search for God.

So be yourself and serve life, as had she.

"Rachel" also serves life by being herself. She is a geriatric specialist, an outreach clinician for older adults. Her job includes driving long distances to meet elderly people reported for some mental-health reason, like hoarding. It can require plenty of creativity to gain their trust and gain entrance in order to gauge the situation and recommend aid services to them.

Over a year ago, alerted to a badly hoarded apartment with a couple in their late sixties or seventies living in an unsafe situation, she went to see them. The report had further stated that the male, his face horribly disfigured, was possibly being abused or neglected and isolated from outside help.

Rachel was to find out.

At the apartment, the male opened the door barely a hand's breadth but didn't invite her in. A woman in the shadows coached him on responses to Rachel's questions.

The woman appeared a trifle paranoid.

Nevertheless, the rules that bound Rachel held that unless people asked for help, she was obligated to leave and not follow up. So she returned to her office and closed the case.

Last month, another report from the Adult Protective Services (APS) on the same couple asked her to open a new case and check on them. Usually Rachel shows up unannounced. This time, however, she called ahead for an appointment.

The woman remembered her. She was very talkative and upbeat. She said that through their church they'd met a wonderful woman who'd been helping them declutter for the past four months and getting them out into the world again.

Rachel was delighted to find the couple's place completely decluttered and organized.

Could Rachel come out to confirm that? Of course. A time was quickly set up.

On the appointed day, the couple were like two completely different people as they excitedly led her into their apartment. Rachel was delighted to find their place completely decluttered and organized. It was quite clean and filled with good feelings.

The friend helping them emerged from a back room, so they all sat and talked for half an hour.

Talk turned to their spiritual beliefs and feelings. Rachel got a nudge. "Do you know about HU?" She explained, "It is the oldest love song to God and a simple and direct way to connect with the positive energy you've been discussing." At this point she mentioned Eckankar. The friend's face brightened, "I was reading an Eckankar book just this morning." She'd drawn it at random from the reading basket by her bed. She had no idea where it'd come from.

All four were humbled by the confluence of events that had graced this day; and for three, learning of HU and Eckankar. Rachel's visit pointed to a sure sign of some divine plan at work.

They all sat and sang *HU* five times.

When she was ready to leave, the three accompanied her to the car. In her mirror, Rachel saw them with arms wrapped around each other, hugging, wearing huge, happy smiles while waving good-bye.

The stories above illustrate two ways to just be yourself yet ready to serve life.

Talk turned to their spiritual beliefs and feelings. Rachel got a nudge. "Do you know about HU?"

A spiritual exercise to help you rise above the blind emotions stirred up by the rigors of the daily grind is this, a very easy one: See yourself as a majestic eagle.

CHAPTER NINE

The Star of
Endless Possibilities

40
Reaching for a Star

*R*obert Browning, the nineteenth-century poet, famously said, "Ah, but a man's reach should exceed his grasp, / Or what's a heaven for?"

Singing *HU* is reaching for a holy star!

An ECKist usually understands that the HU song is simply a love song to God. Just a love song. Not a sneaky way to get a foot in God's door to blurt out a list of gimmes. An exception, of course, would be when an ECKist awakens in some hot water. He is wise to quickly call upon the Master.

Singing *HU* is then quite in order. However, only with the honest attitude of "Thy will be done."

The ECK's will, not ours.

Accept the reality that the Holy Spirit has your best spiritual interests at the forefront. It is likely that the resolution you would want turns out to be something far different.

So whatever the outcome, it is for the best.

Giving and receiving may be likened to the dual action seen in the Audible Life Stream. They are also akin to ocean waves washing ashore, which then retreat to the great body of water that commanded their humble birthings.

Such is the play of God's holy word, the Au-

Singing HU *is reaching for a holy star!*

185

dible Life Current.

This Sound Current is the love and power one can ride home to God. It is the star of endless possibilities. All who sing *HU*, and make a practice of it, have a lot going for them.

The HU song can be our gift to a God seeker. When we share this gift of love with others, then do we also receive divine love in return.

I sometimes reflect upon the fact that my talks and writings are not sermons or philosophical essays for the mind. They are more. Though they touch the emotions and the mind, they aim higher. They reach for Soul.

The Master's teachings enjoy a place where the traditional clergy cannot tread.

People who have had a near-death experience may tell of getting an overview of their life's deeds. Above the physical world's illusions, they clearly saw that what gave them the most satisfaction was hardly what they would have expected.

Was it the garnered wealth, position, or fame? Not at all! It was the small deeds of giving their love and service to others.

That counted for everything!

Let's shift gears now and consider an event reported by Don S., who had attended a recent holistic-wellness fair. A musician, he was asked to stroll the floor among the some three hundred exhibitors, strumming his little dulcimer-like instrument, a Strumstick.

Don wore a colorful robe with a large "Ask me about the HU" button.

People were drawn to the bright sounds of his little Strumstick. Don loves people, so he engaged in light conversations with knots of people. Some

People who have had a near-death experience clearly saw that it was the small deeds of love and service to others that counted for everything!

would ask about the HU. Often, they would even accept a HU brochure or HU card.

He then stopped at a booth where a man was selling a safety product Don was interested in. A woman saw his HU button and asked, "Well, what is HU?"

Before Don could respond, the salesman said, "Oh, I know about the HU! It's great!"

He said he'd been at an event in New York City with seven other people. His team was upset and stressed out. So he told them, "Let's just sing the HU!" They all gathered round and sang *HU*, and everyone calmed right down. They had a great expo.

Don was astonished. This man was not even an ECKist.

"Wait, wait a minute!" the vendor called to the woman. He dug into a duffel bag and produced a bright, little yellow card.

"This is a HU card. Just follow the instructions. It works every time!"

All Don could do was grin and nod his head in agreement.

Does this illustrate a bit the way both a giver and a receiver may be unconsciously giving and receiving the star of divine love?

This dramatic experience gave Don great joy and gratitude, because it was clearly a case where the Master had gone ahead to prepare the way.

The salesman said to the woman, "This is a HU card. Just follow the instructions. It works every time!"

41

The God Power
and the Bishop

*T*he ECK Master Rebazar Tarzs once told his chela Peddar Zaskq (Paul Twitchell) about the latter's need to carry the word of God into the world.

"I am always with you, unto the end of the world."

He went on. "Ye are to carry the word of God into this world, unceasingly and without hesitation. Never be concerned, for I am always with thee, guiding thee and helping thee in every way. My heart goes with thee" (*Stranger by the River*, "The Riddle of God").

And so, Peddar Zaskq went out into the world. This was the beginning of his efforts to attain the ECK Mastership.

Is not every true seeker of God in his shoes too?

In Sweden lives a longtime ECKist who takes her love for the Mahanta, the Living ECK Master into the public arena at every opportunity. The RESA asked Ellenor to represent Eckankar in a panel at a high school. This event was to result

Is not every true seeker of God in Peddar Zaskq's shoes too?

in an important realization for her.

The panel was to consist of seven people: The moderator, three atheists, and three people who had had spiritual experiences. The discussion was to be about the difference between spirituality and atheism.

Most people had a supernatural experience. These are manifestations of the God power.

There had been an investigation of the Swedish people's Christian faith and spirituality that three thousand people had participated in. It revealed that most people had, at one time or another, a supernatural experience. This included telepathy, out-of-body experiences, intuition, a near-death experience, a revelation, guidance from a higher power, or healing. These are manifestations of the God power.

The moderator of the panel was to be a retired bishop who was the director of the body that had ordered the investigation.

Regarding it, he said: "There must be a change in the Swedish order of divine service, an attitude among the priests of listening to the people, instead of telling them what to believe in."

So with that background info, Ellenor asked the Mahanta, the Inner Master, how she could best contribute to the panel.

"Just work on it," he said. She did. However, her preparation did not seem complete.

Then came a second message: make it as simple as possible. Around that time, she had called a friend in Norway, who advised, "Ask Rebazar Tarzs; he is very sharp!"

At bedtime, Ellenor asked the Mahanta and Rebazar Tarzs to tell her what to say on the panel.

The next morning, she knew.

The Mahanta had conveniently placed her at the bishop's left elbow. When it was Ellenor's time to speak, she presented herself as a longtime member of Eckankar. The bishop had not heard of it. She explained that it was the Religion of the Light and Sound of God,* and that one could actually hear the Sound and see the Light!

She further stated that it meant to be a Co-worker with God. This required one to open his/her heart for God every day.

A good, clear, and simple introduction to Eckankar.

The Mahanta then nudged her to speak. A quick sign to the bishop gave her the floor. She told of a princess in Norway who was said to speak with angels. In fact, the princess had even started an angel school. This had upset many Norwegians. But Ellenor pointed out to the panel that the Bible told many stories about angels.

So she posed a question: "Is this just old fairy tales from the Bible, or do angels exist?"

Surprisingly, the bishop jumped in and said, "There are angels! I have met one myself!" Ellenor urged, "Please tell us about that." Modestly, he replied, "Well, I don't know ... "

"But it should be interesting," she pressed, and gave him a little encouraging push with her elbow.

The bishop then told of a time when a strong power had saved his life by lifting him from one place to another, to avoid the rush of an oncoming car. He saw this power as an angel. It was a wonderful story.

Afterward, after she had contributed other

Surprisingly, the bishop jumped in and said, "There are angels! I have met one myself!"

---

* Now, the Path of Spiritual Freedom.

interesting points to the panel discussion, she
handed the bishop an ECK book and a brochure.

A lady then came up to her and said, "You were
the one who had something to say!"

Ellenor realized that to best tell people about
ECK, we must assure them that they are already
in contact with the God power through their dreams,
intuition, and the like.

42

A Dream about
This Article

*F*or several days I'd stewed over this weekend's writing assignment: this article.

That's seldom the case. For most assignments,
ideas come to mind during the week, which I jot
down, because these promptings are like vapor.
They come easily, but they quickly vanish too.

So it was unusual for this article to so trouble
me.

Here's my challenge: how to differentiate my
article from all the excellent stories around mine?
How? A big question.

Little ideas popped up on my mind's screen
throughout the week. How about the nurse who'd
shopped a number of churches before settling on
one where she felt at home, among friends? No,
I'd already done that. A repeat would be stale.

All right, what about the story of captive wild
animals choosing friends that in the wild would
have a standing invitation to dinner? Interesting.
But not this time.

Well, then, how about one on love? I wasn't in
the mood.

*It was
unusual for
this article to
so trouble me.*

So you can imagine how I carried a very uneasy mind off to bed. The night dragged on. Each time I surfaced a moment from sleep—no inspiration yet.

Still I had complete confidence that the ECK, the Holy Spirit, would provide. Hadn't It always?

But why the delay?

Then the ECK spoke! Rather, It showed me in a short, vivid inner experience. Sure, call it a dream if you like.

Then It spoke! Rather, It *showed* me in a short, vivid inner experience. Sure, call it a dream if you like.

I awoke in the other worlds to find myself toting a well-worn copy of *The Shariyat-Ki-Sugmad*, the ECK bible. Some pages had fallen out. So I'd headed for a bookbinder who specialized in the repair of volumes precious to their owners.

Mine *was* dear. Scribbled notes in the margins recalled concepts that fleshed out the text or marked a quote once used in an ECK publication.

The bookbinder studied this patient. "I'll see what I can do."

A week later I returned to his shop. A face like a troubled bloodhound greeted me. "The pages won't stick," he groused. "There's no reason they shouldn't. There's no charge." He brushed away the twenty I tried to hand him. I started for the door.

"By the way," he called after me, "what does the title mean?"

"The Way of the Eternal."

He repeated it. "You know, I read bits and pieces of it while trying to restore the pages to the binding. The pages are thin, but they should have stuck. So why is the book so important to you?"

"It's the holy scriptures of Eckankar." And I

explained about the marginalia.

His head had started at the mention of Eckankar.

"You know," he mused, "I'd never heard of Eckankar until last evening when a friend told me about it. Come back in a week. I'll give it another try."

A week later, his face was a sunflower. "Would you lend it to me for a week?"

"I'd be happy to," I laughed. "But you could have your own copy today. The price is reasonable." He was grateful for a nearby ECK Center's phone number.

"How much do I owe you?"

"No charge. I think I'm coming out ahead."

* * *

And that's how the ECK provided me with the material to write the article you've just read.

A word about the inner worlds: they're real. There are also real events taking place in those very real worlds. So study your dreams. Write them down. I guarantee you'll profit spiritually.

The inner worlds are real. So study your dreams. Write them down. I guarantee you'll profit spiritually.

43
Mission Accomplished

*W*hat title could be more apropos for a successful Vahana endeavor than Mission Accomplished? The following stories show how.

"Jason" once took a job as a bus driver for a private firm. He'd been strapped for cash when he first arrived in San Jose, California, and ended up sleeping in his car. Somehow he learned about a shelter. After about a week of lodging there, the manager assigned him a bed. At bedtime, Jason would sit on his bed, cross his legs, then sing *HU* quietly while contemplating. But that serenity was soon to change.

At bedtime, Jason would sit on his shelter bed, then sing HU *quietly while contemplating.*

A few days later while in contemplation, he noticed someone open the door and leave it open so the hallway light shone upon him. The light filtered through his closed eyelids.

Five days passed. That night he opened his eyes to see Thomas, assigned to the bunk above him, peering in the open door. Two friends of his looked on. Thomas introduced himself later that evening, and the two shared ideas about life and spiritual things.

Unexpectedly, Thomas asked, "Are you the Teacher?"

Jason responded, "No, I'm his messenger."

His bunk mate explained that when he was a child and asked questions of a spiritual nature, no one could give him satisfying answers. Life was good as he grew up. He got a house, a wife, and all the material toys one could ever hope for.

Suddenly, all that changed; he lost everything. Now, this shelter.

One day while in the shower, he finally hit the wall. He gave up. Raising his hands into the air in supplication, with water running down him, he cried out, "I'm tired of this life! Do with me what you want!" He said he just knew the Teacher would come.

Following chapel service a few nights later, Jason showed him and a friend how to sing the HU, after which they discussed dreams. Jason advised them to start a dream journal, an important key to understanding dreams.

Thomas remained certain Jason had come to the shelter just for him.

Jason explained a spiritual principle. "When one cries out to the universe for help," he said, "and is ready to move on spiritually, the universe will send the Teacher. And when the Teacher cannot physically come, he will always send one of his messengers."

Another person at the shelter in dire need of the HU was John. Jason called him "the gatekeeper."

Another person at the shelter in dire need of the HU was John. Jason called him "the gatekeeper." He was in charge of keeping in line the forty or more people at the shelter, getting them to take a shower and finding them a bed for the night.

John was quite upbeat. Yet over the weeks during Jason's stay at the shelter, he noticed the bright light in John's face gradually dim. Uncharacteristically, he began to snap at people. Where had his joyfulness gone?

One morning when John looked much too sad for words, Jason declared, "I have a gift that'll help you. You have a big and important job here at the shelter." So he told John about the HU.

John finally opened his heart. He said his daughter had just lost her battle with cancer and died. Now he was trying to find a way to grieve. Therapy wasn't working. So Jason handed him a HU pamphlet and a copy of the booklet *Spiritual Wisdom on Prayer, Meditation, and Contemplation*.

It was also to be Jason's last night at the shelter. In parting, John shook his hand warmly and said, "I hate to see you go, but I am happy for you. Don't be a stranger!"

Most important, the bright light was again illuminating his face. The Master's mission? Accomplished!

The Vahana experience of "Fallon," however, took a novel turn.

He'd been reading *ECK Wisdom on Life after Death*. That particular morning, he'd placed it on top of his cell phone on a countertop and readied himself for work. Then, about to dash out the door, he grabbed the cell phone and was surprised to find both the phone and the ECK book in his hand. Usually he doesn't carry such books with him. Oh well! He stuck it into his jacket pocket and hurried off to work.

That evening he was to attend an event at a senior-living community. Of the fifty or so people in the room, he knew but two. So he chatted with several new acquaintances.

Most important, the bright light was again illuminating John's face. The Master's mission? Accomplished!

When he was set to leave, he noticed an older woman looking pointedly at him. Both seemed to sense that a conversation was in order.

She mentioned she was a life coach specializing in laughter yoga. Fallon immediately put in, "I'm a member of Eckankar, and I've been doing spiritual exercises for forty years." Thought lines rippled her forehead. Yes, she vaguely recalled hearing of Eckankar and attending some ECK events.

A long and joyful conversation ensued.

The Holy Spirit can do whatever it takes to reach people on the threshold of their next step in spiritual unfoldment.

When the time seemed right, he offered her the ECK book in his pocket. She opened it at random. Flipping through the pages, she was trying to decide whether to keep the gift. A passage that caught her eye read, "Soul exists because God loves It." She read it aloud as if to say, "That's right!"

She accepted the gift.

It later crossed Fallon's mind what the Master might say about this incident: "That's how the Holy Spirit works!" It certainly can do whatever it takes to reach people on the threshold of their next step in spiritual unfoldment.

Then it's mission accomplished all over again.

44
May Thy Will Be Mine

*T*he well-known Lord's Prayer (Matthew 6:9–13) says, "Thy will be done in earth, as it is in heaven." And, of course, it is.

A legacy of the ECK teachings is the practical teaching of how an individual can align the human will with the divine, via the Spiritual Exercises of ECK. Life then becomes easier. That is not to say it becomes easy, for it may not. We are forever facing ourselves.

Long-standing debts come due, even as we are energetically going along accruing new ones, happy, still, in our ignorance tripping upon the toes of a law of life.

Then, woe.

Oh, if we could but learn!

A talk-show host posed a hypothetical question to his radio audience. If you had a choice, he said, of winning a lottery worth millions or having a chance to be twenty-four again, which would you choose? The next question was, why?

Younger callers, those closer to age twenty-four, were more willing to take the money and run. Not too surprising. Even less surprising, perhaps, was

A talk-show host posed a hypothetical question to his radio audience.

201

the number of older callers who said they would gladly be young again, because it would give them an opportunity to get it right the second time around. But would they?

To do so, it would be absolutely necessary to get their will, with all its muddy habits, to line up with the will of ECK (the Holy Spirit), but would they? Could they?

All in the latter group felt assured of success.

By a remarkable coincidence about that time, another radio station featured a story by Nathaniel Hawthorne, nineteenth-century American author, that tied in directly to the question above.

In the story, a small-town scientist has developed a potion to restore youth. He decides upon an experiment. He will collect a handful of the town's oldest people willing to take part in a research project. Each person was known for some glaring failure of character. These shortcomings included vanity, a gossip's wicked tongue, penny-pinching, and such.

They all agreed to take part in the study.

Hawthorne's story sees them all returning to their old ways. All their good intentions fall by the way, with nary a regret.

So it would be a sound bet to say that the radio callers, too, would have learned they were their own worst enemies, helpless to deal with their bad habits.

May thy will be mine.

So easy to say, yet sometimes so hard to do. But if we can manage to do it—oh, the blessings!

Jane was able to attend the 2008 ECK Worldwide Seminar. On October 22, she went to bed determined to be fully aware of inner events that

May thy will be mine. So easy to say, yet sometimes so hard to do. But if we can manage to do it—oh, the blessings!

night, knowing that time has no place in the worlds of God.

Someone called her name after midnight. She immediately sang "Wah Z" and imagined being at the Valley of Tirmer, then actually went there with the Mahanta, who told her to listen with the inner ears. Others were there; she could not make out their faces.

However, Jane was aware of the Rod of ECK Power in the Mahanta's hands, and she sensed a tremendous force coming from it. Beams of energy burst from it. They burst in a pulsing rhythm toward all present.

The bursts filled them with Light and knowing.

Later, still in the inner worlds, scenes of hard economic times floated into Jane's consciousness.

The hard times, she realized, were a spiritual blessing. People would turn again to God. That was the fix. Not a government, not its shortsighted, ambitious plans for a material recovery, but the ECK, the Holy Spirit Itself. It would accomplish Its will. It would accomplish it, in spite of mice or men.

Blessings, blessings all around!

Please try to remember that all which comes your way is to make you stronger spiritually, and stronger in love.

Greater in wisdom, greater in understanding, and greater in compassion.

A spiritual exercise to help you rise above the blind emotions stirred up by the rigors of the daily grind is this, a very easy one: See yourself as a majestic eagle. Catch the wind beneath your wings. Soar upward. Watch the earth and the rainy clouds that cover it now, fall away far, far beneath you.

All which comes your way is to make you stronger spiritually, and stronger in love..

Listen carefully.

Feel the fresh air. See the crystal clear blue sky around you.

Now look up. There is the sun! In its surprisingly soft light stands the Mahanta. Listen carefully. He will give you further guidance.

Better than ever, he realizes now how everything—even a sweet, little lemon tree—needs love to remain healthy.

Chapter Ten

A Sweet Love for Life

45

A Dog and a Cat

"*L*ateef" lives in a small island country. The inhabitants are largely concerned with making it from one day to another, and they are mostly kind to animals.

An exception lived next door.

This country has no animal-protection agency to notify should there be abuse to an animal. People must handle such issues as best they can.

The dog next door howled all day, all night—or moaned, cried, and barked—because it hardly got any food. Also, it was tied to a tree. The landlord said the dog cried because it was starving. The owners worked and had children, but no one bothered to care for the dog. No one. Not even the children.

Lateef is now retired and loves his new home, but "the howler's" carryings-on were really trying his nerves.

The landlord said he'd approached the family about the matter. They flew into a rage.

Lateef had just read in the ECK writings of one's duty to not trespass on others' property. So how could he help the dog? The never-ending racket pushed him into motion. He vowed to help that Soul.

The dog next door howled all day, all night because it hardly got any food. Lateef vowed to help that Soul.

One day, after the family had left for work and school, he decided to get a close look at the dog. It truly was starving. It broke his heart. And since he doesn't eat meat, all he could do immediately was to give it water.

The next day he went to town and bought a bag of dog food.

For several weeks, then, he sneaked next door to feed the dog when the family wasn't home. But he was troubled that, "good deed" though it was, he was still trespassing. It was beyond question.

Finally, he decided to stop trespassing, stop feeding the dog, and turn the matter over to the Mahanta, the Inner Master.

Finally, he decided to stop trespassing, stop feeding the dog, and turn the matter over to the Mahanta, the Inner Master.

He recalled an ECK spiritual exercise which said to write out a spiritual goal or desire fifteen times every day. He wrote: "Mahanta, please change the situation with the barking dog for the good of all."

The second day after Lateef's plea for help, the dog was barking less. Days passed. Sometime in there, the barking had stopped completely.

Still, Lateef kept writing.

Two weeks later he learned of the dog's surprisingly good fortune. The family had given the dog to people who genuinely wanted him, to a place with another dog to play with. He also got food and water. There was a yard to run around in too.

Lateef now understands better what it truly means to give one's cares over to the Master.

Ready for a cat story?

"Nicole" and her husband recently moved from busy, noisy Los Angeles to a small town in the United Kingdom. What an upheaval!

She'd been thrown from working full time to not working at all. From a very active role in the ECK community in California to being nowhere near an ECK Center. She was understandably lonely. And disheartened by too many big changes all at once.

Culture shock.

After a month in the doldrums, she wondered how she could grow spiritually—alone, on a sofa, in a foreign country, and with no job.

One morning, during her spiritual exercises, she pondered this concern. Then she went into the kitchen to make a cup of coffee. While waiting for it to brew, she gazed out the window at a cat in the *far* distance. He was just doing his cat things.

Very softly she said, "Hello, Kitty. Want to come over here and hang out?"

And as if he'd heard, he looked over his shoulder, right at her, and walked the several hundred feet to her front door. When she opened it, there he sat, just looking up at her ever so sweetly with all this love, as if to say, "Hello there, Friend."

She stooped to pet him. He responded by purring and rubbing against her legs, nudging her affectionately.

A fountain of love gushed from this Soul.

Quickly, Nicole heated some chicken for him, the least she could do. But he didn't eat it. He just sat there, satisfied to shower her with waves of love. After some minutes, she hugged him, said good-bye, then went inside.

Quickly, she peeked through the kitchen window. The cat, she discovered, loved chicken too. He was chowing down on it.

So for two months, until she and her husband

Nicole stooped to pet Kitty. A fountain of love gushed from this Soul.

moved to a new home, the cat was a welcome, daily companion as Nicole became acclimated to living in a new country.

Three lessons came from this experience:

First, the love of the Master is always present. She didn't need to be anywhere in particular. Just tuned in.

Second, the cat's desire to love was greater than his desire to satisfy his own needs. The chicken would still be there whether he ate it now or later. By giving of himself, though, he got to give love, receive love and, not to forget, eat the chicken.

Third, she learned that a sweet hunger for God must always come first.

Love, sweet love, for dogs, cats, and all life is essential for our spiritual being.

Love, sweet love, for dogs, cats, and all life is essential for our spiritual being.

46
Love—What Would
We Do without It?

God's love is the food of Soul. We cannot do without it.

Time and again, you tell what it has done for you, how it has changed your life, and how it helps you daily. Tell others who need help your stories. A time of need is the most natural and also most fitting moment to do so.

Everyone and everything needs love.

"Barry" received a potted lemon tree from a neighbor, and he tended it with persistence and loving care. However, unknown to him, it had a bug on the underside of its leaves. He was very careful with the little tree, caring for it with organic remedies and plenty of love. And it flourished, for a while.

Barry's home is at a high elevation, with nights too cold for a warm-weather plant like his lemon tree.

To keep the buds coming and the small fruits growing, he had loaded the potted plant onto a child's wagon, and he'd wheel it into his shop every evening. But due to a health condition, he

God's love is the food of Soul. Everyone and everything needs love.

213

could not bend over to inspect under the leaves for bugs. Asking his very busy wife for help proved futile.

In disgust at his inability to help the little tree, he turned his back on it. He thus withdrew his love and attention.

Barry's disgust quickly turned to dismay.

To his surprise, the tree began to drop its tiny fruit and buds, and even some leaves. He knew the reason. The plant had immediately reacted when he withheld love by walking away from it.

And when its source of love dried up, so did its vitality.

Yet there is a happy ending.

When the tree's source of love dried up, so did its vitality. Yet there is a happy ending.

Barry quickly restored his love and attention to the little lemon tree, and new leaves are once more appearing. Barry jokes, "I am turning over a new leaf."

Better than ever, he realizes now how everything—even a sweet, little lemon tree—needs love to remain healthy.

"Dana" works in an advisory capacity to aid teachers in her school district. Over the years, she has been hounded by fear, unable to lay aside her worries and problems, unable to completely turn them over to the Mahanta for resolution. The Master, Kata Daki, and Prajapati, an ECK Master with a special interest in animals, had all come to her at one time or another to show her how to let go of some cares and fears.

The instruments of choice were cats. Experiences with them had begun to open Dana's heart to divine love in new, unexpected ways.

So as she pulled up to one of the schools and got out of her car, she noticed an orange cat sitting in the middle of the driveway across the street. She wondered offhandedly if this cat was connected to her prior experiences with the ECK Masters and cats.

Dana had been to this school many times and had not seen this beautiful orange cat before. After her meeting, the cat was gone.

However, Dana needed to return to this school later in the day.

In the meantime, she drove to a quiet spot for a spiritual exercise. Things had certainly been difficult lately. All those problems drifting around in her head.

An effective exercise that had helped Dana deal with such troubles in the past was the Snowball technique. To begin, she sang *HU* and wrote all her concerns on a piece of paper.

She then drew a round ball, a snowball, and filled it with her troubles.

Next, in this Spiritual Exercise of ECK, she gave the snowball to the Master, and together they placed it into the ECK Life Stream. There it dissolved. When the exercise was over, she tore up the concerns list and discarded the pieces. The ECK would help her; she was certain of that.

Dana returned to the school refreshed. The cat was not across the street. A few minutes still remained before the meeting, so she shut her eyes for another brief HU.

Just that quick, a thump on the side of the car brought her eyes open. The orange cat, perched on her side mirror, peered in as if to say, Let me in, will you? He jumped in through the open window, crossed to the passenger seat, curled up into a ball, and purred.

The orange cat, perched on her side mirror, peered in as if to say, Let me in, will you?

He showed absolutely no fear.

He was well cared for, he wore a little collar, and his fur glistened. He also sensed when Dana needed to leave. He jumped into the backseat and waited for her to open the back door. Then he made a graceful exit.

Such unconditional love!

What would we do without love?

Dana knew the Mahanta was telling her to keep doing what she was doing and let him take care of her worries, fear, and problems.

And to venture out, to accept the love that comes her way.

What would we do without love?

47

The Mysterious Workings of God's Love

*G*od's love is the operating principle that once created and now sustains all the seen and unseen worlds in existence. And everything and everyone in it. Like you and me.

Love is the tie that binds.

The agent entrusted with the task of returning Souls to the heart of God is the Mahanta, the Living ECK Master. All this you know.

You also know him as the agent of God's love. Friend, counselor, defender, and teacher, he makes things right for you. Be assured that all which enters your life—the good and seemingly bad—is done to reconcile you with yourself. It is better known as working off karma.

This interconnected system of life reveals the way God's love works. The Master stands by to help people realize that love whenever needed.

You well know the ECK tenet of the waking dream. That is, an unusual occurrence in everyday life that offers an insight into some problem. We will give an example to learn from.

"Glen" was to train "Todd," a new hire, to replace

The waking dream is an unusual occurrence in everyday life that offers an insight into some problem.

him at work. Todd was to cooperate with "Fred." However, a rift had developed between them, so tasks that required give-and-take were suffering as a result. Glen was at a loss. How could he get them to get along?

He could try to strong-arm them, but that was not his way.

He could tell his superior about the standoff. No, it was Glen's responsibility. What should he do?

A sure way to resolve the impasse was to jump the chain of command and go straight to the top. So he turned the whole thing over to the Mahanta.

The solution came in two waking dreams, which made Glen put on his thinking cap and fire up his imagination.

The solution came in two waking dreams, which made Glen put on his thinking cap and fire up his imagination. The Master did it this way so Glen could also unfold. After all, what is life about if not to learn and grow spiritually?

Crows—yes, crows—were the players in the first scenario. I am sure they will not mind the use of their real names: Caw, Caw-Caw, and Caw-Caw-Caw.

The first two crows were making an awful racket. In fact, it had been their squabbling that drew Glen's notice in the first place.

Caw held a large piece of food in his beak. Caw-Caw stood off casually to one side, too far to be an immediate threat. But Caw knew that kind: greedy and full of envy. Caw-Caw needed to be taught a good lesson. Scolding was not doing it.

So Caw dropped his food. Flying and skipping along the ground, he attacked Caw-Caw with beak and thrashing wings.

Caw-Caw-Caw then swooped down amid the confusion and flew off with the morsel.

So Caw and Caw-Caw got none.

Glen observed the outcome.

The second waking dream took place at home the next morning. He was in the kitchen making coffee for his wife. The filter he was about to place in the coffee machine seemed too thick. Ah, two filters were stuck together in an inseparable manner.

Unfazed, and frugally minded, he used the doubled filter anyway, for the same pot of coffee.

The following day, Glen met with Fred and Todd to review the previous day's work. It was substandard. Their lack of cooperation was responsible.

"I respect both of you too much to give you advice," he said. "So I'll tell you two stories. You can make of them whatever you want, and I will not bring this matter up again." Glen told his waking-dream stories, then he walked out the door.

An hour later, the one who had been the real obstructor called Glen with an apology. He had risked both his and the other's careers in the company.

The workings of God's love? Not so mysterious, really.

And so two waking dreams had restored God's love to Glen's workplace.

The workings of God's love? Not so mysterious, really.

48

It's Always about People and the Love They Carry

*I*n *Stranger by the River*, the ECK Master Rebazar Tarzs is instructing Peddar Zaskq, his student, on a fine point of divine love.

"The requirements of growth," he says, "demand that you exert the greatest degree of love for what is perfectly in accord with Soul. Our highest happiness will be best attained through our understanding of, and conscious cooperation with, the divine law."

Rebazar continues, "It is love that imparts vitality to our minds and hearts and enables it to germinate. The law of love will bring to you all necessity for your spiritual growth and maturity."

With that in mind, I present to you my article from the September 2012 *RESA Star*. Notice the spiritual hunger of the seekers.

Also see the ways the ECKists were open channels for divine love.

Notice the spiritual hunger of the seekers. Also see the ways the ECKists were open channels for divine love.

* * *

The pastor of a Minnesota church said, "Really, people are looking for relationships today . . .

221

a place that's vibrant and full of faith. You can almost walk into a church and tell it's there."

A very perceptive man. His religious group is the fastest growing in the state.

Relationships, yes, but more precisely, it's all about love. Sheri at the ECK Spiritual Center (ESC) passed on stories from a few calls from people new to ECK. Their stories will illustrate the reason your Vahana work matters so much in your region.

By the way, when Sheri gets one of these special calls, she turns her chair to face a picture of the Master on her desk.

The first caller was a First Initiate. She had moved into a new area and was destitute, homeless, and alone. She wanted counseling. It was explained that we instead offer ECK Spiritual Aide sessions. She had done that. But Sheri listened.

The woman spilled her troubles, adding that she had been a Catholic, and they called it the dark night of the Soul. That is where she was now.

"We call it the same in Eckankar," Sheri said.

About to end the call, Sheri looked up from the computer to the Master's photo again. A thought flashed to her.

About to end the call, Sheri looked up from the computer to the Master's photo again. A thought flashed to her. She said, "What sets Eckankar apart from other religions is that it gives us the tools we need when we face difficulties. One of the main tools is gratitude."

The caller's voice brightened. She, too, had a lot of things to be grateful for and began to list them, including the beautiful place she was in, with nature all around.

At call's end, she said the big difference in Eckankar was the love she felt.

Another caller was a man who had first heard

of Eckankar the previous night. He and his wife were in town because their daughter had gone there for medical treatment. He was out of work for forty days. Until his daughter was admitted to the hospital, he had to pay for all their room and board. A truly heavy burden.

So the previous night he had called for a taxi. The cabbie said he could not come immediately, but that he would send another driver.

The taxi arrived. The driver saw that the man was carrying a heavy burden. The former said it was no coincidence the first cabbie could not come, which made it necessary for him to fill in.

He told the couple about HU and handed them a HU card, and played a recording of the HU song. The caller felt a sense of peace and calm come over him as he listened to the HU. The driver had told him that it would be a good idea to call the ESC.

So the caller did, the next day.

Prior to bed, he said, he quietly sang *HU* while his wife listened. He slept through the night for the first time in months and woke up feeling that everything would be OK.

He asked Sheri, "How can I use HU for things to get better?"

She explained, "HU is undirected prayer. It allows everything to come into its rightful place." At some point she also said, "When we sing *HU*, we open our hearts to receiving love, and singing *HU* is an act of love."

Stepping back to take in the whole picture, Sheri observed that somewhere in Texas is a taxi driver introducing people in need to the HU. She felt fortunate to have heard about the profound

Prior to bed, the man quietly sang HU while his wife listened. He woke up feeling everything would be OK.

impact of this act of love on one man.

Isn't it always about people and the love they carry?

49
Love in All Its Splendor

*T*oday we'll look at two stories. The first is gritty—a graphic, high-risk event in the life of an ECKist. The second story is gentler, more soothing. However, both reflect the divine love that makes life worth living.

Here we go.

The first story takes place in West Africa, where "Dr. Asis Kwei" is a medical specialist. And, notably, she is also an ECKist. One of her daily routines is to play ECK recordings on her drive to work, especially on Fridays, a special day, one for doing a spiritual fast. This particular recording told of the Master having to overcome the fear of death. Her thoughts about his dramatic confrontation? Well, of course, he was in training for the ECK Mastership.

But her own life was about to meet a similar crisis. She'd never, ever imagined such a thing could possibly happen to her.

Inwardly, she reminded the Master about a recent promise he'd made to appear to her in his radiant form. He reassured her, "I'm still coming." Upon her arrival at the hospital for work, she was quickly swallowed up by her duties. She was on call.

Inwardly, Dr. Kwei reminded the Master about a recent promise he'd made to appear to her in his radiant form.

About 8 p.m., the lights in the call room were dimmed to save electricity. She decided to drive to the intensive care unit (ICU) of the medical campus to study for an upcoming medical exam. There, the lights were always kept on bright to handle emergencies.

As she parked, two men with drawn guns confronted her. She was told to climb back into her car and lie down in back. Silently she called on the Master for help; he quickly confirmed his presence. Yet her plight seemed impossibly grim.

The two men drove a long time through the night. When the car finally stopped, she was blindfolded, and one of the men led her into the bush while the other drove off in her car. Her escort tried to rape her but decided it was not the right time of month for that. So nature spared her that horror.

Next, he forced her into a small, dark room in the bush that boasted only a tiny window. In the darkness she discovered another female; it was that woman's second day of captivity. Her family scraped together the ransom, and she was set free later that very night.

Asis felt sure her kidnappers had no such intentions in mind for her. They'd probably kill her. She had recognized one of the crooks as a security guard at the hospital, so they dared not let her live.

In response to her numbing fear, the Master still said not to worry. He would see her safely through the night.

In response to her numbing fear, the Master still said not to worry. He would see her safely through the night. Understandably, she continued to be afraid.

Then, about 3 a.m., both Wah Z and Rebazar Tarzs appeared to her in their radiant bodies. She voiced a desperate cry for help. She kept chanting, "Wah Z, Wah Z, Wah Z!" Z smiled and said, "I'm with you."

No sooner had he spoken than she heard a sharp crash against the door, then gunshots and scuffling. She kept chanting. Wah Z had stayed with her during the shoot-out.

The next moment, a foot kicked her as she lay on the floor. "Who are you?" a voice barked. "I am Dr. Kwei," she replied. Men helped her struggle to her feet. She was safe. They were the police.

Asis ends her report: "I am sincerely grateful to the ECK. I LOVE THE ECK." Small wonder.

Let's now switch to a more soothing and restful story.

"Jamie" stopped at the local trash dump, because her area has no pick-up service. It's a bring-your-own-trash (BYOT) kind of place.

To her surprise, a chicken strutted boldly around the dump grounds. The attendant said it'd just turned up one day, a few weeks ago. So he'd fed it and then built a little house for it. The chicken was happy. It greeted people dropping off their waste.

Jamie observed, "It looks like she's your entertainment during the day."

One day, not so long ago, a man dropping off trash had exclaimed, "Hey, that's my chicken!" But he turned aside the attendant's offer to return it to him. "The other chickens won't let her eat. You're welcome to her."

She was of the Ameraucana breed, whose eggs are a beautiful pastel green, like dyed Easter eggs.

The man mused, "You ever seen anything like that? They're good, so I eat 'em."

Jamie stopped at the local trash dump. To her surprise, a chicken strutted boldly around the dump grounds.

To Jamie it seemed a kind of love story. The attendant has company all day, and the chicken has a home. "The ECK is taking care of things just right," Jamie decided.

These two stories tell of love in all its splendor.

Sheila asked Wah Z for a sign that her mom was OK. In response, a spectacular shooting star lit the sky. Sheila had the answer her heart had longed for.

CHAPTER ELEVEN

Blessings Large and Small

50
Sweet the Moments
Rich in Blessing

"*M*oments" fascinate me.

In our country church the congregation sang a hymn with a line I especially liked, "Sweet the moments rich in blessing." An uplifting song. The people liked the melody because it let them sing with gusto.

Lately, my attention has strongly been directed toward the sacredness of THIS MOMENT. The ECK teachings speak of it as the Here and Now.

We are never more alive than at THIS MO-MENT. Past moments? Now just memories, since the actual moments are no more. That said, they may leave residue—karma—to be worked on later. On the other hand, our expectations of some future event may leave us cheerful, indifferent, or even fearful.

We are never more alive than at THIS MOMENT.

Past and future moments toy with our emotions, although they're not real. Much like fog, past and future moments have little substance and have either vanished or are still to appear.

Let's consider how past, present, or future occurrences play out in the following story. Practice awareness. Notice how the story's moments glide into each other.

"Donna," an H.I. from the Midwest US, is a Vahana, an ECK missionary. She doesn't own a car, so she rides the bus. Over the years she's made a number of bus friends. Donna is also responsible for getting the Master's seminar talks aired on the local cable-access TV station. So she's often at the library, where the TV station is housed too.

The library is currently switching equipment from DVDs to a newer technology. So content from DVDs must now be uploaded first. One DVD was taking longer to upload than usual, when the Inner Master nudged Donna to walk out from the recording room into the library hall.

There was "Debra," a bus friend. After they'd spoken at length, Donna remarked that she was a member of Eckankar; she also mentioned the HU song.

To Donna's surprise, Debra already knew about the HU song. At a Christian church she attends in town, she saw someone passing out HU cards. Moreover, she'd also seen the HU mentioned in a Catholic church bulletin. Donna was dumbfounded.

Next, Donna showed Debra the little book *ECK Wisdom on Life after Death*. No longer should it have been surprising to hear Debra declare she already owned the book. "Two Afro-American girls gave it to me at an afternoon event where free hot dogs were handed out." The Inner Master had clearly gone ahead.

But Debra offered a final morsel. A HU card turned up at a Burmese apartment complex in town. How that woman did get around!

Donna and others on the Vahana team scratched

their heads. Involved as they were in most all the missionary activity in the area, they thought they knew about every Vahana effort in the small community. They were surprised and baffled. None knew of any ECKists who'd have been at those places doing what Debra had related.

As far as they knew, there were no ECKist Afro-American girls nearby. They were delighted, of course, certain that ECK Masters were their benefactors.

Throughout this story, I hope you watched how one moment turned into another, and then another. Moments, of course, go on all the time. Nothing profound there. Life is a virtual stream of moments that flow continuously in the sea of life.

But know the ECK does turn a spotlight on at certain moments. When that lights up, you are at the fullness of your present state of consciousness.

All children of Divine Spirit seek to be open to such sweet moments rich in blessing.

All children of Divine Spirit seek to be open to such sweet moments rich in blessing.

51
The Mahanta Helps with Her Mother's Translation

*W*e come, we go, for such is the way of life.

Translation, death, is an initiation. As surely as we are born, so surely must we die. Translation spares no one. Each event is an occasion of wonder, though Soul may this time be entering a heaven that has been Its home so many times before.

We now hear the beautiful story of the passing of "Sheila's" mother. Many lessons and insights abound throughout it.

Sheila's mother, "Mary," did not believe in God. Of a skeptical, scientific bent, her credo was straightforward: if you can't see it, don't believe it. Yet in her eleventh hour of life, she began to awaken to the inner realities.

For example, she felt the presence of her long-departed mother in a nearby room. She told Sheila, "I feel so much comfort."

Sheila answered, "You know, Mom, that's Grandma waiting for you on the other side." She

Sheila's mother, Mary, did not believe in God. Yet in her eleventh hour of life, she began to awaken to the inner realities.

237

knew Mary realized that herself, but acknowledging the fact was very hard, for it meant her mom would soon be gone. Theirs was a close, loving relationship in spite of a huge difference in their beliefs and practices.

Theirs was a close, loving relationship in spite of a huge difference in their beliefs and practices.

Sheila was an ECKist; Mary, an atheist.

A health practitioner, Sheila used energy medicine and acupuncture to assist healing. Mary was in favor of traditional medicine, yet she would sometimes let Sheila treat her, out of love and respect.

Their love bond was very strong.

Mary's health had recently undergone a marked deterioration. Her eyesight was mostly gone. So, of course, the pleasure of reading had forsaken her too. Congestive heart failure was a concern. Her balance was unsteady, leaving her afraid to walk. And there was the blood disorder, which impaired red-blood-cell production. On top of all that, she also had liver cancer.

It is little wonder she was ready to go.

Sheila and her husband left for a conference. Upon their return, they headed straight for the emergency room, because Mary had just been admitted there.

During her weeklong stay in the hospital, Mary began to lapse into dementia. Sheila tried an energy technique on her, time permitting. This brought Mary back; the dementia disappeared.

Then Mary was transferred to a nursing home, where the staff tried to rehabilitate her. But she largely refused food and drank little water. Nor could she walk.

A week in the nursing home produced no improvement.

Plans had been made, however, to keep her there. Fortunately, during a lucid moment, Mary announced she wanted to go home, a relief for Sheila. She had often promised her mother she would not let her spend her last days in a nursing home. She belonged at home. There, Sheila could be with her and care for her.

And so it was.

A benefit of Mary's imminent passing was that the whole family was together again. Mary was often away in the other worlds, however. She was then unaware of being at home.

Sheila knows that Wah Z, the Inner Master, is always on hand to help ECKists and their dear ones. So for days on end, she would sing, "HU . . . Wah Z." And into her mother's ear, she would whisper, "Look for the man in the blue suit," or, "Look for the Blue Light!" Then, Sheila would feel the Master's presence ever so strongly.

Sheila knows Wah Z, the Inner Master, is always on hand to help ECKists and their dear ones.

"Do you see Wah Z?"

"Do you see the man in the blue suit?"

When Mary would nod, Sheila was in her cheering section. And so more days passed. But why was it taking Mary so long to translate? The doctor and Sheila's dad both noted that people who took so little nourishment usually died a lot quicker than Mary was. She had hung on for a month.

Sheila decided to ask the Mahanta about this.

He said, "It's necessary for her to live a while longer. There are many inner preparations to make first, so that you can be at her side during the transition. That's because she's not an ECKist."

In due time, the preparations were all complete. Sheila then had three dreams. In the first, she left her body and walked into the room where her mother's hospital bed was set up. She stood alongside it. Her mother reached up and took hold of her neck so Sheila could help her out of the body.

A second dream showed both of them on the Mental Plane. On the horizon, beyond a beautiful body of water, they saw five or six moons that shimmered with gold and shades of orange, blue, and red. They were breathtaking!

The third dream showed Mary being greeted by a large circle of friends. She translated that coming evening.

Later, Sheila went outside into the fresh night air. She asked Wah Z for a sign that her mom was OK. In response, a spectacular shooting star lit the sky.

Sheila had the answer her heart had longed for.

A second dream showed both on the Mental Plane. Five or six moons shimmered with gold and shades of orange, blue, and red. Breathtaking!

52
Divine Connections

*D*ivine connections. They are of all kinds.
Sometimes we come to an understanding of these spiritual connections early, other times late. No matter. It is vital, though, to make them. Isn't that the point of the ECK teachings?

Following are stories from two ECK chelas featuring these divine connections.

For the previous two months, "Lil" had struggled to understand the reason for sudden bouts of severe nausea. She suspected a supplement. It made no sense, however, as there was no pattern.

What was the real reason?

On a Thursday morning, there it was again. When she later arrived at the office, she wondered how to cope once the others came. She decided to lie on the sofa a few minutes. Maybe the nausea would let up.

She breathed deeply to relax, then shut her eyes, listening to music playing on her computer.

Lil then gazed into her Spiritual Eye.

"Mahanta," she whispered, "please help me. Is there anything I need to know?"

Recently, she'd heard of the "dump truck" technique. One loaded all concerns and questions into

Lil gazed into her Spiritual Eye. "Mahanta," she whispered, "please help me. Is there anything I need to know?"

this truck and then dumped them at the Master's feet. Lil liked to handle her own problems. She'd long thought that situations cropping up in her life were hers alone to deal with.

Or so she'd once thought.

The ECK Master Fubbi Quantz suddenly appeared in her Third Eye. He was in a healing room at the Katsupari Monastery in northern Tibet. Lil was there with him but here, too, still on the couch.

It seemed Lil was connected to the heavens above, while also in her physical body below. A beautiful blue light shone.

After a few minutes there came a lifting sensation. She felt lighter. It seemed she was connected to the heavens above, while also in her physical body below. Then it felt as if she were being stretched to link heaven and earth.

A beautiful blue light shone. She relaxed, letting the ECK Master help with her spiritual connection. All trust was in him and this Blue Light, the Mahanta.

Five minutes later, a car door slammed in the parking lot. A coworker would be in the office within seconds. Lil sat up. Thirty minutes, still no nausea. She realized the nausea had made her too physically connected and weighed down on this plane.

She'd been out of balance. It was first necessary to heal her spiritual connection.

The rest of the day went far better. By nightfall, she was even ready to dance. The next day saw more energy pour into her.

This healing left her able to again pursue her mission of writing.

A connection made.

Now let's hear from "Gail," a homeopath. You may remember her from an earlier *Mystic World* article. Health issues had kept her from continuing her outer ECK activities, so she made ECK CDs, books, and brochures easily available in her office.

One day there came a desperate call. The caller was in the final stage of cancer and given only five months to live. She made an appointment.

Gail dreaded that day to come. What could she offer apart from listening, and to give emotional support and maybe some remedies for the woman's body?

The dreaded day came all too soon.

Gail felt unwell and shamefacedly hoped the lady would not show, though the ECK had been nudging her to see her. Soon the outer door opened. She heard the woman take a seat in the waiting room. Gail really was unwell now and hardly in a frame of mind to deal with this case.

The consultation began.

"How are you going to handle this emotionally, mentally?" Gail asked. "How have you been handling it?"

The patient replied, "I'm going to sing *HU*." A matter-of-fact declaration.

"HU. So you know about HU?"

"No," she said, "but when I came in, I sat down and prayed to God to show me what to do next to help myself. You have a little book on your table about love being the cornerstone of life.

"I flipped it open, and it said something like 'Sing *HU* when you need help.' So I'm going to sing *HU* because God told me to!"

She asked how to sing *HU*. Gail led her through five minutes of singing, then gave her a HU CD. She was thrilled. And as she was leaving, she walked over and hugged Gail.

"I just remembered," she added, "years and

The patient said, "I'm going to sing HU because God told me to!"

years ago I heard of Eckankar and HU, but I didn't bother. I guess God has taken me full circle to bring the HU back to me in the last moments of my life. I am going to play the HU CD all the way home, and every night and every morning."

When she had left, Gail just sat down and cried. She thought, *How could any ECKist ever take credit for what the ECK does?*

Her patient has not returned, but she did call to say she was doing well. It had been eight months. Better than five.

And she still sings *HU* every morning and every night. It's her divine connection.

Her patient still sings HU *every morning and every night. It's her divine connection.*

53
That One-on-One Feeling

*N*early ten years earlier, "Clara" had returned to Germany. The move took her to the former Communist part of Germany where any mention of the word "God" would bring down an iron wall.

Her loneliness was overwhelming.

She had met lots of people, though, thanks to her dog, Tell, a great communicator who loved everyone. However, she missed the company of the ECK community and her very active role in it.

Where could she turn for comfort?

She decided to ask the Mahanta to put her to work on the inner planes. Could she also attend ECK Satsang or a book discussion there? Anything to be with ECKists!

And so it began.

On the inner, the Mahanta provided her with an opportunity to clean classrooms, participate in ECK seminars and book discussions, and even teach a children's Satsang. This latter task later led to an outer meeting with one of the children in class.

The class contained twelve kids of about age

On the inner, the Mahanta provided Clara with an opportunity to teach a children's Satsang. This later led to an outer meeting with one of the children.

245

four. When the bell signaling the end of class rang, all the children jumped up and ran from the room, happy to be free. But one little girl stayed. She looked truly sad.

Clara gently asked, "What's the matter, Lena?"

"When I'm here everything is fine," the girl replied, "but in the morning at home, I forget everything. How will I ever find the Mahanta?"

Comforting her, Clara said, "The Mahanta will find you. He knows where you are every moment."

Time rolled on.

A few months later, Clara received an invitation to a great-grandniece's first birthday party. And who'd also come? Lena and her mother. The child flew toward Clara, hugging her and calling her by name. So happy to meet Clara on the physical plane, she'd been completely blind to a possible reaction from her mother.

"How come you know each other?" her mother demanded. Lena looked at Clara a bit frightened.

"We have met before—right, Lena?" Relieved, the child nodded. Clara represented the Mahanta's link to Lena. This outer meeting confirmed the validity of Clara's inner experiences. The Mahanta had given both her and Lena an unforgettable one-on-one feeling that countless ECKists have also known.

The Mahanta had given both Clara and Lena an unforgettable one-on-one feeling that countless ECKists have also known.

Another case in point is an event "Scott" and "Sara" dealt with, each from a unique point of view. The two were involved in a duck incident, which is getting to be a familiar narrative for ECK readers. But there is a catch. Several years passed before either learned of the other's role.

So what happened?

It's uncertain who originally saw the duck and

her brood trapped against the concrete divider of a four-lane highway. Scott likely drove past them first. He'd been moving with the flow of heavy traffic when he spotted the duck family in the little narrow band of concrete alongside the roadway. But of necessity, he swept by. It would certainly have caused an accident had he tried to pull over.

Thinking quickly, he doubled back at the next light and took a frontage road back to see if anything could be done to help the duck and ducklings. To his surprise, a miraculous, long break in the traffic flow occurred just then. The timing was perfect. Quickly, he shooed the mother duck and her brood back across the road to the safety of bushes on the other side of the roadway.

To Scott's surprise, a miraculous, long break in the traffic flow occurred just then.

Sara told her story at an Eckankar Spiritual Center discussion class. A number of groups were formed, and Scott happened to fall into the same group as Sara. As Scott related his story, she felt relief to hear his part in the ducks' dilemma.

Then she told the group her story.

She'd been on the same road, the same day as Scott, and had also seen the ducks. Immediately, she began to sing *HU* and asked for the Mahanta's aid, if it could be given. For the same reason, she immediately called the 911 emergency number.

However, the person answering the phone said they didn't do ducks. They only handled more urgent emergencies.

Sara kept singing *HU*. But now she also shifted into high gear, calling upon Wah Z and all the ECK Masters, including the renowned Prajapati. The latter has taken a special interest in animals.

In her heart, she saw the ducks reach the side of the road, safe from harm.

Still, she was left with the awful feeling she should have done more to help the ducks. When Scott told his story, her heart skipped a beat with a flood of joy. The ECK had heard her plea and sent Scott. That's how she saw it. The Mahanta had intervened in the natural order of things to demonstrate the power of love.

Stories like these leave ECK dream travelers with a confirmation of their own one-on-one experiences with the miracles of ECK. They know that what they've just read bears the clear ring of truth.

ECK dream travelers know that what they've just read bears the clear ring of truth.

54

Love Letters to the Mahanta

An initiate report is a love letter to the Mahanta. I love to read them. They often speak of ways the ECK, Holy Spirit, has brought help or understanding to a situation.

Outwardly, the incidents may appear minor. But scratch the surface, and they reveal the wonders of divine activity.

"Ada" understands that the true value of writing her ECK initiate report every month, in a diary, is a love letter from the heart. What is the benefit? It is one of the easy ways to gain spiritual unfoldment and resolve karma. So she tells stories of unconditional love.

Here's one:

"Kathe," a close friend who was not an ECKist at the time of Ada's report, had a strong feeling of resentment toward her older sister. She felt her sister had an overbearing attitude.

Then, out of the blue, after twenty years of silence, her sister dropped in for a visit. The reunion was a disaster.

The reunion was a replay of the same misun-

Ada understands that the true value of writing her ECK initiate report every month, in a diary, is a love letter from the heart.

249

derstandings and power plays of old. Kathe didn't understand that old family karma was knocking at the door. Karma? Kathe had not known about it. So Ada filled her in. She also offered a spiritual exercise.

Kathe was to inwardly invite her sister into her living room and ask her to please listen to what Kathe had always wanted to say. She would ask the Mahanta to sit by her side while speaking.

She was to remain calm. There were to be no accusations. Nor would she interfere in her sister's psychic space. Kathe was to practice unconditional love. For the first time, she expressed her point of view concerning their troubled relationship. It was an immense relief to so be unburdened.

Then, unexpectedly, her sister called some days later, asking for another meeting. There, they finally made a reconciliation.

Let's leave Ada and Kathe now and take a look at "Mike" and "Jane" on vacation.

They had looked forward to a four-week stay by the seashore. However, a few days before departure, Mike's exuberance on a rebounder left him too ill for travel. He ended up in bed for a week, recuperating. Instead of canceling the trip, they cut the vacation to three weeks.

It's noteworthy that they were able to reschedule the plane tickets, hotel, and car rentals for a week later, without penalty. They even saved money avoiding a week of hotel and car-rental fees.

The sea air revitalized their health. About every time they went to a restaurant, they were able to share info about the ECK, over and over.

All too soon, it was time to return home.

They were at the airport, waiting to board. But

the airline had overbooked. Would they be willing to sign up on a list of people ready to give up their seats? They mulled it over. Mike and Jane couldn't decide, since their son was to meet them at their destination.

But Jane put their names on the list anyway.

Behind them, an elderly couple was frantic. They were traveling standby. They wanted to reach Minneapolis in time for a good friend's ordination into the priesthood the following morning. Now their flight was overbooked.

Mike and Jane identified themselves as ECK clergy. The old man went into a rant about Catholic church history.

Minutes sped by; flight departure was near.

Jane suggested a quiet prayer, and surrendering the situation to the Holy Spirit. He ignored her. The plane was boarding.

Jane spoke up. "Do you know how to surrender? We need to do that now!" He was taken aback, but he and his wife shut their eyes. Jane made an outer declaration of turning the situation over to the will of the Holy Spirit.

Mike and Jane did an inner HU.

The airline had filled its overbooking problem with other people first on the list to give up their seats. But two more seats were needed for this standby couple.

The Catholic couple mentioned Mike and Jane's names to the ticket agent. An instant later, they began to board. They flashed Mike and Jane quick smiles and a thumbs-up, which were returned. They had made their flight.

Of such are the love letters I receive.

Of such are the love letters I receive.

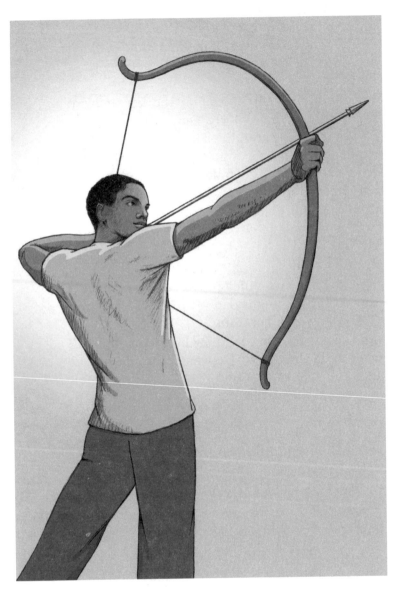

Tony tells of a strong desire to move forward in his spiritual unfoldment: "I need to pull the arrow further back." This is the Call of Soul.

CHAPTER TWELVE

The Journey Home

55
Pull the Arrow
Further Back

"Tony" tells of a strong desire to move forward in his spiritual unfoldment, and he refers to it with a rich, evocative expression: "I need to pull the arrow further back."

This is the Call of Soul. It urges one to pack up and move on to Its spiritual goal.

Tony had lately been thinking a lot about divine love, gratitude, surrender, and being a vehicle for ECK in every moment. He tells a story.

A couple of months ago, a footstool had broken in his home. He finally dismantled it, but there it lay on the floor for a week, until late one afternoon when he got a nudge to repair it. Though he did not much feel like doing it then, he nevertheless decided to follow through on the nudge.

At a home-supply store, he met an employee who asked him pleasantly, "Can I help you?"

It truly seemed he wanted to be of service. Tony remarked on his good attitude, and the man replied, "I am grateful for this job." Tony then told of how gratitude had been much on his mind, too, so he tried to remember to be grateful every day for all

The Call of Soul urges one to pack up and move on to Its spiritual goal.

255

the blessings in his own life.

The other's response was positive. Tony thus knew of a certainty that the ECK was in action.

Tony then handed him a screw from his stool. The employee said, "Follow me." And while walking along, the man told of a recurring dream. It was about his being a Jewish elder in a family in danger of being killed, and he had given his life to protect them.

An immediate insight hit Tony: the dream was of the Holocaust! The employee said there was no one to tell his dream to.

"They'll think I'm crazy!"

Tony assured him that many people share such dreams of a possible past-life experience, himself among them. The fellow then explained how he had migrated from the Philippines with his family some eight years ago.

It was turning into a good spiritual conversation. More was still to follow.

Hoping for a chance to tell of ECK, Tony asked for an item whose location he knew. Then he told about HU and the protection this ancient name for God offered when sung. Moreover, he said he would bring him a HU card after checkout.

The fellow insisted on helping carry the purchases to Tony's car. Tony gave him a HU card as promised.

Then Tony noticed in the backseat a brand-new copy of *Past Lives, Dreams, and Soul Travel*. He passed it to the grateful employee. An exchange of smiles, and each was again on his own way.

Pull the arrow further back. Tony did, and so also did the nanny "Kate" hired.

Kate and her husband had plans to attend

Tony assured the employee that many people share such dreams of a possible past-life experience, himself among them.

their state's ECK regional seminar. She wanted a nanny to help manage their two children while she and her husband went to different events. So she and the nanny spoke by telephone one evening to become acquainted. Until then, no mention of ECK had been made.

The nanny's favorite uncle, it turned out, had died fifteen years earlier; he had been an ECKist. A week ago, she had posted a notice on Facebook that simply read, "I need the universe to send me divine guidance."

Kate began to laugh. The nanny wanted to know why. So Kate reeled off a string of "coincidences." First, the nanny had asked for divine guidance; she was interested in spiritual things; believed in reincarnation; and loved her uncle, an ECKist.

The list ended with Kate's revelation that this overnight stay was to be at an ECK seminar.

Surprised, the nanny blurted, "You're an ECKist?" Kate assured her it was indeed so. The nanny reflected. "I think the universe is giving me a gift." Then she added that her eight-year-old son had said, "Life and love are all about Light and Sound."

The Mahanta had seen her pull the arrow further back, wanting to again move forward in her spiritual life. For that reason, he opened a way.

The two seekers here thus benefited from the Master's love. Please keep an eye out for seekers and pull your arrow back further too.

The Mahanta had seen the nanny pull the arrow further back, wanting to again move forward in her spiritual life. For that reason, he opened a way.

56

Yes, Heart-to-Heart Connections!

I originally wrote this article for High Initiates, Brothers of the Leaf. Consider that as you read it, and you will find keys for your journey to Self-Realization and God-Realization.

*　*　*

"Farah" likes to meet people who come to the ECK Temple and to give tours when called upon to do so.

One day while she was driving, the Golden-tongued Wisdom came to her through a radio ad mentioning "heart-to-heart connections." She did, indeed, want that quality of contact with people, especially seekers. So she decided to be sincerely interested in their stories when life drew them together. She wanted to open herself.

With that in mind, she said to the Mahanta, "Please help me make heart-to-heart connections with whomever I see at the Temple today, especially visitors and seekers, so I can share the message of ECK from the bottom of my heart."

Such was her "prayer."

As you read this article, you will find keys for your journey to Self-Realization and God-Realization.

259

At work, near closing, a woman of around thirty wanted a tour. Farah obliged her. The visitor, it turned out, had lived in the area for many years, yet this was her first time at the Temple. Happy, open, and curious about Eckankar, she listened eagerly to Farah's explanations of the ECK principles. Then she concluded she planned to make it to a Temple event.

At that moment, Farah knew the heart-to-heart connection had been made. The visitor's eyes had lit with a childlike characteristic: Soul's deep yearning to know more.

So she continued saying this prayer every morning.

A few days later, a Canadian woman paused at the information sign in the foyer and began to read a brochure on display there. The sanctuary was open; she could have gone right in. Then Farah got a nudge to invite her into the reception area.

The two chatted. The other happened to be of Iranian descent, so they switched to Farsi, since Farah spoke it too. The woman had just moved to the Minneapolis area with her husband, and she'd gone online to search for spiritual places in the area. That's how she ended up at the ECK Temple. She wanted a tour. The paintings in the vestibule impressed her, for she could see the truth of the Light and Sound of ECK shining through the artwork. And she liked the peacefulness in the paintings.

She was a true seeker and an independent thinker. Expressing a concern about sanctifying a human being and considering him a holy person, she felt a bit more comfortable when Farah ex-

The visitor's eyes had lit with a childlike characteristic: Soul's deep yearning to know more.

plained, "In Eckankar, we respect our spiritual leader but will never worship him." She went on to speak of the HU CD, on which he invites the listener to try a spiritual exercise, but only if it feels right.

He also cautions one not to be a blind follower just because someone had told them to be so.

The visitor seemed very pleased to hear that. She, like all truth seekers, did not like the idea of giving up her spiritual freedom. Yes, she did wish to attend an upcoming Temple class for the public.

Farah's heart-to-heart prayer had helped another Soul along Its way home to God.

Soon after, she asked the Mahanta a specific question. "How," she wondered, "can I be the best I can possibly be at this moment?"

Back at work, she noticed four young men approaching the Temple. They wanted a tour. She explained the Temple was closed for the day but invited them to come back that evening at seven o'clock, when they could look around. They turned to leave. It occurred to her to ask, "As long as you're here, do you have any questions?" Questions, they did! The questions ranged from the length of time she'd worked there to what the basic teachings of Eckankar were.

Throughout the whole connection with the young men, Farah had felt her answers were coming from a deep, secure place within her. She remained very focused in the moment, calm, and was just herself. "I felt I was talking with my friends," she recalled, "not necessarily with four nineteen-to-twenty-year-old Mormon missionaries."

They were curious about the ECK materials. At her invitation they took info packs, copies of

The visitor seemed very pleased to hear that. She, like all truth seekers, did not like the idea of giving up her spiritual freedom.

ECKANKAR's Spiritual Experiences Guidebook, and HU CDs.

Before their departure, she posed a final question. "What do you like about your religion?" she wanted to know. The group's leader reflected a moment, then replied, "That's a good question. It's just like you said about the ECK. Our religion helps us in our daily lives, too, and helps us learn from different experiences."

In looking back, Farah was amused that though they had announced themselves as missionaries, they hadn't made any kind of missionary effort.

Take to heart the points made here and, perhaps, fine-tune your own conversations with the Master.

57

A Closer Look at the ECK Initiations

An ECK youth, eligible for the Second Initiation, hesitated to take it. Her fear was that it would be too rough. She, no doubt, wanted my assurance that facing herself would be easy. But an ECK initiation is all about facing oneself. She lacked the self-confidence to do so.

The Mahanta, the Living ECK Master is highly unlikely to wave a magic wand and sprinkle the stardust of self-assurance upon one.

After all, the purpose of this life is to gather up experiences. That is the only track to spiritual unfoldment.

Long ago, during the Vietnam War, the draft was in effect, prompting me to enlist in the air force before the army could nab me. I was scared. Could I, a dropout from a divinity college, hope to measure up to basic training? I had serious misgivings. One hurdle after another was cleared, and soon, there I was, at Lackland Air Force Base in Texas.

Basic training *was* hard! However, I found that I could hold my own among the sixty men in my

An ECK youth, eligible for the Second Initiation, hesitated to take it. She, no doubt, wanted my assurance that facing herself would be easy.

flight. Yes, I made a few big bloopers, which the two training instructors took some pleasure in, trying to reduce me before my fellow airmen. But I stuck with it, not taking their bullying to heart.

It was a relief when the ire of an instructor turned aside to another airman. Together, and individually, I and everyone in my unit grew more self-reliant over the six-week course.

All throughout basic training, we had heard of the awful obstacle course. It was a washout threat. Anyone failing it would face the disgrace of not measuring up and be sent home. We all feared that course.

To my surprise, I did well there. I crossed the finish line among the first four or five of sixty men. That served as a tremendous boost to my self-esteem.

In a way, the obstacle course, like an ECK initiation, meant facing up to one's mistakes and doing things a better way.

In a way, the obstacle course, like an ECK initiation, meant facing up to one's mistakes and doing things a better way.

The ECK youth afraid of taking her Second Initiation needs a few more everyday experiences to grow comfortable with taking that all-important spiritual step of the Second. I told her not to worry. The Mahanta would let her know when the time was right. At some point she will be eager to advance spiritually, for she, like every ECK initiate, must accept the Master's invitation at her own pleasure.

The timing of that choice is all her own.

Tests and challenges that accompany an initiation usually run from mild to average. However, on occasion an initiate meets more of the lower self than he or she would like.

"Tim" offers one such example.

In mid-August, he received his Sixth Initiation. He became ill with a flu in September, which led to a secondary infection in the external lung lining, which caused a breathing difficulty. During this entire period, a terrible fear of death dogged him. He had entered a cave of purification on the Sixth Plane.

This was a dark night of Soul. It let him see how his certainty of having overcome the grip of materialism was just an illusion.

Tim believed he had moved beyond a fear of losing his material body, or a desire for material achievement. But he was wrong, so wrong. All the same, he kept faith with the Mahanta, the Living ECK Master and knew that this intense purification was pushing out a stack of negative karma.

His outer self was struggling to find a balance, even as the inner being was engaged in seeking a spiritual balance too.

The outer side, his human self, was simply reflecting the efforts of the spiritual self to restore a closer bond with the Inner Master, which had suffered as materialism had become too important to Tim. Tim could have put off the challenge. But he chose to go forward and face his misguided direction.

At the height of his terror, a voice spoke from his depths.

It was the voice of the Mahanta.

It was the ECK Itself!

It said It had never left him throughout his countless lives. It loved him now, and It always had.

Moreover, he could never die. He would always have life, freedom, joy, and the power to be, because

He would always have life, freedom, joy, and the power to be, because the ECK was him, and Tim was It.

the ECK was him, and Tim was It.

Further, he was to love himself, really love himself. All the way.

That is what each ECK initiation is about.

58

The Unstoppable ECK

$\mathcal{T}$he Holy ECK flows like the Stream from Sugmad (God) that It is. It is the Voice of God. It permeates all life, for It is Life Itself.

Is it any wonder, then, that this elixir can relieve any and all conditions? This Divine Stream is the unstoppable ECK.

A radio station recently did an interview with a well-known guitar player. The interviewer asked about the way the guitarist performed onstage. Did he suffer from stage fright? (Not for years.) How did he divide his attention between the audience and his playing? (It varied. Sometimes, it was too much on his audience and too little on his playing. The result was a so-so performance.)

Did other factors distract him? (Very much so! He would be completely absorbed in the music, when his mind would think about his breakfast of bacon and eggs. Then, just like that, he'd come to again onstage. The shift in time and space threw his playing off badly.)

And what about illness?

(Oddly, said the guitarist, he often played his best when he was the sickest.)

Is it any wonder that this elixir can relieve any and all conditions? This Divine Stream is the unstoppable ECK.

Why? (He then was no longer self-conscious. Then, he became the music itself.)

He was then at his clearest.

The very same thing is true of a clear ECK Vahana. He gets out of his own way. He does not let self-consciousness keep him from doing the thing he knows the Mahanta wants done. But how to go about it?

To be an open, clear instrument for the divine energy of ECK means to remove all filters from one's state of consciousness. No fears. No self-doubts. Please be assured that the Master has gone on ahead of you. He has already tilled the ground, sown the seed, fertilized, and watered it.

Here is one such case. Back in 1989, "Halim" was in Europe, having a hard time keeping body and Soul together. He was at his wit's end. Lack of food and other basics of survival caused him fear and pain, but the spiritual door was about to open.

One night, there came a strange, perplexing dream.

He saw a boat. In it were three men. Two were dressed in clothes of Jesus's time; their hair was black.

The third man's appearance was quite apart from that of the other two. He was a figure in all white. His hair was white, as were his beard and robe. In his hand was a basket. It was full of bread.

"Take some bread!" the man in white said.

Halim did as he was bidden, taking several pieces.

The man was of a highly striking appearance, and Halim asked people around him, "Who is he?"

"Jesus!" said two of Halim's fellow travelers.

The Master has gone on ahead of you. He has already tilled the ground, sown the seed, fertilized, and watered it.

"Impossible!" replied Halim. "Jesus has no white hair and beard."

"Nevertheless," they insisted, "it is so." And there the matter rested for five years without a resolution.

In 1994, since Halim was in Europe, his brother-in-law asked a favor of him: to buy some videotapes of an Eckankar event.

Halim told him, "I have never, ever heard this name. Are they a new sect?"

His brother, still in their home country, laughed, and said, "Just buy me some tapes and send them home to me."

So Halim bought some videos and decided, out of curiosity, to watch them before shipping them home. They provoked his interest and curiosity. In response to Halim's request to learn more about Eckankar, his brother-in-law sent him some ECK books. In one was a picture of the man in white, the ECK Master Fubbi Quantz.

This quiet, yet mysterious, holy man had provided Halim with bread, which was both the material and spiritual food that Halim stood in such desperate need of. It had taken five years to learn his name.

In 1995, Halim became an ECK chela.

The unstoppable ECK! In the most incredible way, It had reached out and tapped Halim's shoulder with the golden scepter of life.

The Master, for he is this Spirit of Life incarnate, had prepared this seeker gradually for the eternal teachings of ECK.

Step out courageously. You'll see miracles too.

Many stories can be, and are, told of how the Master goes on ahead of the ECK Vahana.

Step out courageously. You'll see miracles too.

59
Do with Me As You Will

Should someone ask, "Would you do anything at all for the Holy Spirit?" you would say, "Of course, I would!"

But what if it meant a complete change in your way of doing nearly everything?

Recently, the ECK did just that for me. It placed me in the middle of dozens of health professionals, like a game piece on a board. Yet what an opportunity! Meeting so many unfamiliar with ECK was a chance to demonstrate and explain what ECKists are and believe.

When Faye, a registered nurse, asked about my special diet, she was visibly relieved to learn it was founded on nutritional needs rather than some religious quirk.

Faye, you might appreciate, has done a lot of living. As a former waitress, she abhorred the food one of our friends cooked and delivered to us.

"How can you possibly eat that?" she demanded.

Feigning a look of hurt surprise, I offered to share my meal with her. Her face screwed into a knot of disgust.

"I'm going out for a greasy cheeseburger, coffee,

Recently, the ECK placed me in the middle of dozens of health professionals, like a game piece on a board. Yet what an opportunity!

and fries," she said. "Don't stuff yourself!" I raised my spoon in parting.

When I first arrived at the hospital, word had quickly spread that a broken-hip injury, from a fall on black ice, had come in—and it was the leader of Eckankar. But Faye, a member of the Assembly of God church, was determined to be the complete professional. No biases. Faye would give her all. So, she later said, she hooked up her nose a notch and marched into my room. It was love at first sight. She is a kindred spirit.

She had once driven a long-haul semitrailer, then survived spinal meningitis during pregnancy, was currently also a deputy county sheriff, and had too many other sidelights to her life to possibly mention here. A Soul rife with karmic experiences.

Some of her coworkers did not understand our easy banter. They often chided her for her lack of respect.

But I left her supervisor a glowing commendation about her healing laughter, care, compassion, and understanding. A dear, sweet Soul; we had met again. It was every bit a spiritual reunion.

Do with me as you please.

Again, the ECK had done with me as It would, to better touch Souls ready for the exciting journey home to God. Would suffering a broken hip have been my first choice to serve God? Surely not. It sometimes takes a stiff upper lip to serve the Divine Power. Rest assured, though, our retuning for Its purposes is generally far more agreeable than an experience similar to mine.

Holly is another of many healers who deserves recognition and special thanks. A physical therapist

Would suffering a broken hip have been my first choice to serve God? Surely not. It sometimes takes a stiff upper lip to serve the Divine Power.

with two school-age children, she is upbeat and humble. And funny in an apologetic way. When asked about a husband in her family, she glanced at her calendar-watch and smiled. "Tomorrow at this time our divorce will be final."

A talented teen slalom skier, she once ranked sixth or seventh in her age-group in the nation. Impressed, I exclaimed, "That's great!" She shrugged indifferently, "I guess." For her, the past is past; the present is busy enough. Dear Holly.

Lori, a beautiful woman too, is a bundle of pure ECK energy. An occupational therapist, she gives praise and a thumbs-up to every patient who clears some small hurdle. Though her heart is in helping patients in recovery, she nevertheless has outside interests. She is an avid bear, deer, elk, small-game, and fowl hunter. A cougar once stalked her and her husband. But Lori does not hunt cougar: it is a trophy animal. She hunts for meat.

Who could not love her? Lori is always kind but determined to help patients better yesterday's scores.

Who could not love her? Lori is always kind but determined to help patients better yesterday's scores.

Dora swept into our life like a West African wind. In fact, she hailed from Ghana. A nurse's aide on the night shift, she routinely brought ice for my hip and relayed messages to the shift's registered nurse to bring the pain medication.

But Dora did more, much more. When the pain became nearly unbearable, she laid a warm, encouraging hand on my shoulder. Her eyes, too, said, "I understand."

The day of my discharge, she said she would see us the coming night as usual.

"We're leaving today," Joan said softly.

Dora stopped. She came back and surrounded

*Spirit of all
living things, I
live to hallow
Your name. Do
with me as
You will.*

the two of us with a hug as warm as all Ghana. "Maybe I'll come see you in Chanhassen," she said in parting. We look forward to the day.

Here ends my tribute to a few of many beautiful people in the healing field.

And, Spirit of all living things, I live to hallow Your name among lost and wandering Souls. So do with me as You will.

About the Author

Award-winning author, teacher, and spiritual guide Sri Harold Klemp helps seekers reach their full potential. He is the Mahanta, the Living ECK Master and spiritual leader of Eckankar, the Path of Spiritual Freedom. He is the latest in a long line of spiritual Adepts who have served throughout history in every culture of the world.

Sri Harold teaches creative spiritual practices that enable anyone to achieve life mastery and gain inner peace and contentment. His messages are relevant to today's spiritual needs and resonate with every generation. *Kirkus Reviews* comments, "The powerful optimism of these teachings should resonate with all readers, even those unacquainted with ECK."

Sri Harold's body of work includes more than one hundred books, which have been translated into eighteen languages and won multiple awards. The miraculous, true-life stories he shares lift the veil between heaven and earth.

In his groundbreaking memoir, *Autobiography of a Modern Prophet*, he reveals secrets to spiritual success gleaned from his personal journey into the heart of God. Find your own path to true happiness, wisdom, and love in Sri Harold Klemp's inspired writings.

Next Steps in Spiritual Exploration

- **Browse our website: www.Eckankar.org.**
  Watch videos; get free books, answers to FAQs, and more info.
- **Attend an Eckankar event** in your area.
  Visit "Eckankar around the World" on our website.
- **Explore advanced spiritual study** with the Eckankar discourses that come with membership.
- **Read additional books** about the ECK teachings.
- See "Contact Eckankar" page 281.

Advanced Spiritual Living

Go higher, further, deeper with your spiritual exploration!

ECK membership brings many unique benefits and a focus on the ECK discourses. These are dynamic spiritual courses you study at home, one per month.

The first year of study brings *The Easy Way Discourses* by Harold Klemp, with uplifting spiritual exercises, audio excerpts from his seminar talks, and activities to personalize your spiritual journey. Classes are available in many areas.

Each year you choose to continue with ECK membership can bring new levels of divine freedom, inner strength to meet the challenges of life, and direct experience with the love and power of God.

Here's a sampling of titles from *The Easy Way Discourses*:

- In Soul You Are Free
- Reincarnation—Why You Came to Earth Again
- The Master Principle
- The God Worlds—Where No One Has Gone Before?

BOOKS

You may find these books to be of special interest. They are available at bookstores, online booksellers, or directly from Eckankar.

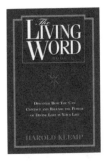

The Living Word, Books 1, 2, and 3
Harold Klemp

The spiritual truth and divine love in Sri Harold's timeless articles from the *Mystic World* and *Eckankar Journal* show us how we can plan for and achieve tangible growth.

Wisdom of the Heart, Books 1, 2, and 3
Harold Klemp

Three decades of Wisdom Notes, *Mystic World* letters from Sri Harold to the ECKists, teach new and practical ways for you to live the spiritual life to its fullest potential.

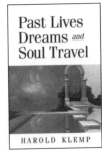

Past Lives, Dreams, and Soul Travel
Harold Klemp

These stories and exercises help you find your true purpose, discover greater love than you've ever known, and learn that spiritual freedom is within reach.

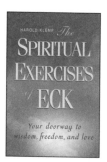

The Spiritual Exercises of ECK
Harold Klemp

This book is a staircase with 131 steps leading to the doorway to spiritual freedom, self-mastery, wisdom, and love. A comprehensive volume of spiritual exercises for every need.

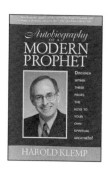

Autobiography of a Modern Prophet
Harold Klemp

This riveting story of Harold Klemp's climb up the Mountain of God will help you discover the keys to your own spiritual greatness.

Those Wonderful ECK Masters
Harold Klemp

Would you like to have *personal* experiences with spiritual masters that people all over the world—since the beginning of time—have looked to for guidance, protection, and divine love? This book includes real-life stories and spiritual exercises to meet eleven ECK Masters.

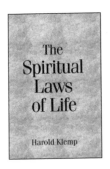

The Spiritual Laws of Life
Harold Klemp

Learn how to keep in tune with your true spiritual nature. Spiritual laws reveal the behind-the-scenes forces at work in your daily life.

The Shariyat-Ki-Sugmad, Books One and Two

The "Way of the Eternal." These writings are the scriptures of Eckankar. They speak to you directly and come alive in your heart.

Spiritual Exercises for the Shariyat, Book One and Spiritual Exercises for the Shariyat, Book Two
Harold Klemp

The secret doctrine is the portion of the Shariyat-Ki-Sugmad that the Mahanta passes to the chela by means of the Spiritual Exercises of ECK. Every exercise in these two books is a portal to greater self-mastery, higher consciousness, more clarity in your thoughts and life-direction. Golden wisdom for you!

ECK Essentials
Harold Klemp

Your keys to spiritual living. These ECK essentials from the Master nourish, guide, uplift, heal, reveal and strengthen the desire and resolve of Soul to reach Its sacred goals. Open your heart to the Master, and you will hear inner, secret whispers of truth.

Available at bookstores, from online booksellers, or directly from Eckankar: www.Eckankar.org; (952) 380-2222; ECKANKAR, Dept. BK135, PO Box 2000, Chanhassen, MN 55317-2000 USA.

CONTACT ECKANKAR

For more information about ECK or ECK books, or to enroll in ECK membership you may:

• Visit www.ECKBooks.org

• Enroll online at "Membership" at www.Eckankar.org (click on "Online Membership Application"), or

• Call Eckankar (952) 380-2222 to apply, or

• Write to:
ECKANKAR, Dept. BK135
PO Box 2000
Chanhassen, MN 55317-2000 USA

GLOSSARY

Words set in SMALL CAPS are defined elsewhere in this glossary.

Arahata An experienced and qualified teacher of ECKANKAR classes.

Blue Light How the MAHANTA often appears in the inner worlds to the CHELA or seeker.

chela A spiritual student, often a member of ECKANKAR.

ECK The Life Force, Holy Spirit, or Audible Life Current which sustains all life.

Eckankar *EHK-ahn-kahr* The Path of Spiritual Freedom. Also known as the Ancient Science of SOUL TRAVEL. A truly spiritual way of life for the individual in modern times. The teachings provide a framework for anyone to explore their own spiritual experiences. Established by PAUL TWITCHELL, the modern-day founder, in 1965. The word means Co-worker with God.

ECK Masters Spiritual Masters who can assist and protect people in their spiritual studies and travels. The ECK Masters are from a long line of God-Realized SOULS who know the responsibility that goes with spiritual freedom.

Fubbi Quantz The guardian of the SHARIYAT-KI-SUGMAD at the Katsupari Monastery in northern Tibet. He was the MAHANTA, the LIVING ECK MASTER during the time of Buddha, about 500 BC.

God-Realization The state of God Consciousness. Complete and conscious awareness of God.

HU *HYOO* The most ancient, secret name for God. It can be sung as a love song to God aloud or silently to oneself to align with God's love.

initiation Earned by a member of ECKANKAR through spiritual unfoldment and service to God. The initiation is a private ceremony in which the individual is linked to the Sound and Light of God.

283

Kal Niranjan   The Kal; the negative power, also known as Satan or the devil.

Karma, Law of   The Law of Cause and Effect, action and reaction, justice, retribution, and reward, which applies to the lower or psychic worlds: the Physical, Astral, Causal, Mental, and Etheric PLANES.

Kata Daki   A female ECK MASTER, who, like all others in the Order of the Vairagi, serves the SUGMAD by helping others find the MAHANTA, the LIVING ECK MASTER. Her pet project is to help people get back on their feet during hardship.

Klemp, Harold   The present MAHANTA, the LIVING ECK MASTER. SRI Harold Klemp became the Mahanta, the Living ECK Master in 1981. His spiritual name is WAH Z.

Living ECK Master   The spiritual leader of ECKANKAR. He leads SOUL back to God. He teaches in the physical world as the Outer Master, in the dream state as the Dream Master, and in the spiritual worlds as the Inner Master. SRI HAROLD KLEMP became the MAHANTA, the Living ECK Master in 1981.

Mahanta   An expression of the Spirit of God that is always with you. Sometimes seen as a BLUE LIGHT or Blue Star or in the form of the Mahanta, the LIVING ECK MASTER. The highest state of God Consciousness on earth, only embodied in the Living ECK Master. He is the Living Word.

Peddar Zaskq   The spiritual name for PAUL TWITCHELL, the modern-day founder of ECKANKAR and the MAHANTA, the LIVING ECK MASTER from 1965 to 1971.

planes   Levels of existence, such as the Physical, Astral, Causal, Mental, Etheric, and SOUL Planes.

Rebazar Tarzs   A Tibetan ECK MASTER known as the Torchbearer of ECKANKAR in the lower worlds.

Satsang   A class in which students of ECK discuss a monthly lesson from ECKANKAR.

Self-Realization   SOUL recognition. The entering of Soul into the Soul PLANE and there beholding Itself as pure Spirit. A state of seeing, knowing, and being.

Shariyat-Ki-Sugmad   The sacred scriptures of ECKANKAR. The scriptures are comprised of twelve volumes in the spiritual worlds. The first two were transcribed from the inner PLANES by PAUL TWITCHELL, modern-day founder of Eckankar.

Soul The True Self, an individual, eternal spark of God. The inner, most sacred part of each person. Soul can see, know, and perceive all things. It is the creative center of Its own world.

Soul Travel The expansion of consciousness. The ability of Soul to transcend the physical body and travel into the spiritual worlds of God. Soul Travel is taught only by the Living ECK Master. It helps people unfold spiritually and can provide proof of the existence of God and life after death.

Sound and Light of ECK The Holy Spirit. The two aspects through which God appears in the lower worlds. People can experience them by looking and listening within themselves and through Soul Travel.

Spiritual Exercises of ECK Daily practices for direct, personal experience with the Sound Current. Creative techniques using contemplation and the singing of sacred words to bring the higher awareness of Soul into daily life.

Sri A title of spiritual respect, similar to reverend or pastor, used for those who have attained the Kingdom of God. In Eckankar, it is reserved for the Mahanta, the Living ECK Master.

Sugmad *SOOG-mahd* A sacred name for God. It is the source of all life, neither male nor female, the Ocean of Love and Mercy.

Temples of Golden Wisdom Golden Wisdom Temples found on the various planes—from the Physical to the Anami Lok; chelas of Eckankar are taken to these temples in the Soul body to be educated in the divine knowledge; sections of the Shariyat-Ki-Sugmad, the sacred teachings of ECK, are kept at these temples.

Twitchell, Paul An American ECK Master who brought the modern teachings of Eckankar to the world through his writings and lectures. His spiritual name is Peddar Zaskq.

Vahana The ECK missionary; a carrier of ECK or the message of ECK.

vairag The spiritual virtue of detachment.

Wah Z *WAH zee* The spiritual name of Sri Harold Klemp. It means the secret doctrine. It is his name in the spiritual worlds.

For more explanations of Eckankar terms, see *A Cosmic Sea of Words: The ECKANKAR Lexicon*, by Harold Klemp.

STORY INDEX

INDEX

Bibliography

"Anger and Arrogance Meet Humility." *The Mystic World*, December 2013.

"Being Enthusiastic, Positive, and Giving Freedom." *The Mystic World*, June 2007.

"Be Yourself and Serve Life." *Eckankar Journal*, 2018.

"Can Karma Be Managed?" *The Mystic World*, June 2017.

"A Closer Look at the ECK Initiations." *The Mystic World*, September 2010.

"Connections." *The Mystic World*, September 2011.

"Divine Connections." *The Mystic World*, March 2015.

"A Dog and a Cat." *The Mystic World*, December 2015.

"Do with Me As You Will." *The Mystic World*, September 2012.

"A Dream about This Article." *Eckankar Journal*, 2016.

"Explorations in a Rocking Chair." *The Mystic World*, September 2008.

"Faith, Love, and Trust." *The Mystic World*, December 2011.

"A Few Good Stories from You." *The Mystic World*, June 2015.

"Gifts, Gifts, and More Gifts." *The Mystic World*, March 2007.

"Gifts of Love." *The Mystic World*, December 2006.

"The God Power and the Bishop." *The Mystic World*, June 2010.

"Growing Pains." *The Mystic World*, September 2015.

"Helping the ECK Is Helping Yourself." *The Mystic World*, December 2007.

"Help on the Spot." *Eckankar Journal*, 2011.

"In the Spiritual Garden." *Eckankar Journal*, 2009.

"Is There a Fresh Way to Say . . . ?" *The Mystic World*, March 2016.

"It's a God Thing." *The Mystic World*, June 2016.

"It's Always about People and the Love They Carry." *The Mystic World*, December 2012.

"The Joy Blotters—Bringers of Doubt and Fear." *The Mystic World*, June 2011.

"Learning about ECK." *Eckankar Journal*, 2015.

"Lemuria, Atlantis, and Today." *The Mystic World*, September 2007.

"Life Deals Our Cards Facedown." *The Mystic World*, June 2014.

"Like My Brother Duane." *The Mystic World*, June 2009.

"Love in All Its Splendor." *The Mystic World*, December 2017.

"Love In, Love Out." *The Mystic World*, December 2014.

"Love Is a Many-Splendored Thing." *Eckankar Journal*, 2010.

"Love Letters to the Mahanta." *The Mystic World*, March 2014.

"Love—What Would We Do without It?" *The Mystic World*, March 2011.

"The Mahanta Helps with Her Mother's Translation." *The Mystic World*, March 2008.

"May Thy Will Be Mine." *The Mystic World*, September 2009.

"Mission Accomplished." *The Mystic World*, September 2017.

"The Mysterious Workings of God's Love." *The Mystic World*, March 2012.

"Open Your Heart, Then Your Eyes and Ears." *The Mystic World*, December 2009.

"Pain and Heartache from Long Ago." *Eckankar Journal*, 2017.

"Peace in Our Time—or Ever?" *Eckankar Journal*, 2007.

"Problems and Their Resolutions." *The Mystic World*, December 2008.

"Pull the Arrow Further Back." *The Mystic World*, December 2010.

"Reaching for a Star." *The Mystic World*, June 2013.

"Resist God's Will?" *Eckankar Journal*, 2014.

"Serving a Snapping Turtle—and Others." *The Mystic World*, September 2013.

"Serving You!" *The Mystic World*, March 2010.

"A Shake-Up, Caffeine, and Some Birds." *The Mystic World*, March 2013.

"A Structure to God's Love?" *The Mystic World*, March 2009.

"The Sun of God's Love in Their Lives." *Eckankar Journal*, 2012.

"Sweet the Moments Rich in Blessing." *The Mystic World*, December 2016.

"That One-on-One Feeling." *The Mystic World*, March 2017.

"'That's Irrelevant!'" *The Mystic World*, June 2012.

"These Simple Miracles." *The Mystic World*, June 2018.

"This Is the Gift!" *Eckankar Journal*, 2008.

"The Unstoppable ECK." *The Mystic World*, June 2008.

"What about the Expressions of Consciousness?" *The Mystic World*, September 2014.

"Yes, Heart-to-Heart Connections!" *The Mystic World*, September 2016.

"Yes, We Can Reach All Seekers!" *The Mystic World*, March 2018.

"Young or Old, It Does Not Matter." *Eckankar Journal*, 2013.